The European Reformation 1500–1610

Alastair Armstrong

Series Editors
Martin Collier
Erica Lewis
Rosemary Rees

Heinemann

Heinemann Educational Publishers
Halley Court, Jordan Hill, Oxford OX2 8EJ
Part of Harcourt Education

Heinemann is the registered trademark of
Harcourt Education Limited

© Alastair Armstrong 2002

First published 2002

ISBN 0 435 32710 0

04
10 9 8 7 6 5 4 3 2

Designed, illustrated and typeset by Wyvern 21 Ltd, Bristol

Printed and bound in Great Britain by The Bath Press Ltd, Bath

Index compiled by Ian D. Crane

Photographic acknowledgements
The authors and publisher would like to thank the following for permission to
reproduce photographs:
AKG: 4, 31, 40, 41, 45, 58, 69, 95 (left), 125, 153; Bridgeman Art Library: 3,
116, 164; British Museum: 88; Hulton Getty: 10, 36, 78, 91, 121 (all), 154;
Mary Evans Picture Library: 12, 76, 95 (right), 145; Studio Wilfried Kirsch: 20,
24

Cover photograph: © AKG

Picture research by Liz Moore

Dedication
To my Mother and Father

CONTENTS

How to use this book   iv

PART 1 AS SECTION: The European Reformation, 1517–63   **1**

Introduction   1
1 What was the nature of the pre-Reformation Church in Europe?   2
2 What was the nature of Lutheranism?   16
3 What were the reasons for the success of Lutheranism?   34
4 How did Lutheranism consolidate and expand?   49
5 The Radical Reformation: Zwingli and the Reformation in Zurich   61
6 What is the significance of the Anabaptists and John Calvin?   66
7 The Catholic Reformation   74
AS Assessment 1   106

PART 2 CROSSING AS/A2 SECTION: The French Wars of Religion and the expansion of Calvinism in France, 1540–1610   **113**

Introduction   113
1 How, and with what opposition, did Calvinism grow in France?   114
2 What are the main features of the French Wars of Religion, 1562–98?   120
AS Assessment 2   132

PART 3 A2 SECTION: Calvin and Calvinism to 1572   **135**

Introduction   135
1 How successfully did Calvin establish a Reformation in Geneva?   136
2 How did Calvinism develop in the rest of Europe?   151
A2 Assessment   168

Bibliography   170

Index   171

HOW TO USE THIS BOOK

The book is divided into three parts: an AS section; a crossing AS/A2 section; an A2 section. Each part has been written in a distinct style.

The AS chapters are written as a descriptive analysis. The key aspects of the European Reformation are tackled in these chapters. The questions at the end of each chapter aim to challenge the students to use the information in the chapter to analyse, prioritise and explain the important aspects of the subject. It is hoped that, by reading each chapter, discussing key issues and answering the summary questions, students will acquire a clear understanding of each topic.

The crossing AS/A2 section explains the main features and debate about the French Wars of Religion. It is written in such a style as to appeal to AS students studying AQA option B unit 3 and to those studying Edexcel unit 4 option 2b: Calvin and Calvinism to 1572. There is an assessment section at the end of this part to help students tackle AS course essays on the subject.

The A2 section of the book is more analytical in style. It deals with the themes and issues of the period that are included in the awarding bodies' specifications. Students who use the book as part of their A2 studies should also read through the relevant chapters in the AS part of the book. An example of this is that students who are studying Calvin and Calvinism at A2 level should not only read Section 6 but also Part 3 of the book. The A2 part is written in such a way that it should also prove useful for AS students who wish to extend their understanding of the subject.

There is an assessment section at the end of each of the three parts. These sections include exam-style source and essay questions for each specification. There then follows detailed guidance on how students might answer the questions, together with sample answers.

PART 1: AS SECTION

The European Reformation, 1517–63

INTRODUCTION

This part of the book traces the development of the Reformation in Germany between 1517 and 1563.

By 1563 the religious landscape in Germany had been irreversibly altered by the actions of Martin Luther and his followers. In 1500 the Catholic Church had been one of the institutions which bound German society together. Yet as a consequence of the Religious Peace of Augsburg in 1555, the foundations had been laid for a Germany whose inhabitants could choose between two Christian faiths. Clearly it is important that we understand the role of the Catholic Church in society and the anti-clerical attitude which prevailed over much of Germany and some other parts of Europe in 1517. Reformers and humanists had challenged the doctrine of the Catholic Church before Luther came along, but none of them gave birth to a significant movement. Therefore we must examine not only the individuals, but also the environment in which they operated if we are to explain the success of Lutheranism in Germany. Moreover, it will also be important to identify the limitations of Lutheranism, and chart its relatively conservative progress after 1530 in the hands of the princes. Finally, we must take into consideration the effect which political and socio-economic factors had on the development of the Reformation, and gauge the significance of Lutheranism with regard to the emergence of a 'modern state' in Europe.

CHAPTER 1

What was the nature of the pre-Reformation Church in Europe?

Introduction

In 1500 there was only one faith in western Europe, namely Catholicism. At the head of the Catholic Church was the **Pope residing in Rome**. The Church played a central role in the lives of the vast majority of ordinary people. Their loyalty and devotion can be seen in the large amounts of money left to the Church in wills or the considerable sale of **primers** and prayer books. However, one must be careful not to generalise and, in some parts of Europe during the early sixteenth century, the Church was seen to be failing in its spiritual duties. **Abuses** were prevalent within the late medieval Catholic Church, although the extent of corruption varied, as did the extent to which the people cared about the corrupt practices of some high-ranking clergymen.

The state of the Church c.1500

It is possible, however, to outline two interpretations of the state of the Catholic Church on the eve of the Reformation.

- One interpretation views the Catholic Church as being on the brink of collapse: a church so riddled with abuses and corruption that it could no longer cater for the spiritual needs of the people. In short, a church in need of reform but incapable of or unwilling to reform from within its own structure. This line of argument certainly has its advantages in that it neatly explains **Martin Luther**'s success: a German reformer faces an inadequate Catholic Church – no contest.

However, history is rarely that straightforward.

- A second line of argument presents a Catholic Church in a relatively healthy state: a church that generally fulfils the needs of the people and operates effectively despite

KEY TERMS

The Pope in Rome The Catholic Church regards the Pope as the successor of St Peter (head of the Apostles) and, as such, he has full and supreme power of jurisdiction over the Church in matters of faith and discipline. Indeed, the Pope is regarded as infallible on most matters of faith and morals. That is to say that any doctrinal decision he makes is binding on the whole Church. The Pope is elected by a college of cardinals and sits at the top of a strict hierarchy consisting of cardinals, archbishops, bishops and priests. During the early modern period, the Pope had great political power and influence, in part as a consequence of the Papal States in Italy over which he ruled.

Primer A primer was a devotional book that included the psalms and the litany of saints. Dating back to the fourteenth century, primers were often seen as religious textbooks to teach and instruct children and adults alike.

Abuses Abuses should be seen as the corrupt practices of the Catholic clergy. An example of an abuse might be the buying or selling of a clerical post or title, known as simony.

Martin Luther by Lucas Cranach the Elder.

KEY PERSON

Martin Luther (1483–1546)
Born the son of a copper miner in Eisleben in 1483. He attended school at Magdeburg and Eisenbach before studying at the University of Erfurt from which he graduated in 1505. The next three years were spent at an Augustinian monastery at Erfurt. In 1507, Luther was ordained as a priest and in 1508 he entered the University of Wittenberg where, in 1512, he became Professor of Biblical Exegesis, a post he held until his death. Before this appointment, in 1510, Luther visited Rome, where he reported on the corrupt practices of the Catholic Church. It was during this mission that Luther encountered the practice of indulgence selling, the criticism of which formed the basis of Luther's 95 Theses in 1517. Luther is rightly regarded as the father of the European Reformation due to the way in which he successfully challenged the Catholic Church.

isolated cases of ill behaviour and ignorance among the clergy; a church linked to the people socially, religiously and economically. In short, a thriving church.

As is so often the case, the historian must look to find a middle ground on this issue. Undoubtedly, the corruption of the Catholic Church has been over-exaggerated in the past. However, one thing is clear: by 1555, the Holy Roman Empire was bi-confessional (two faiths were being practised: Catholicism and Protestantism). From a religious perspective, the old belief of 'one faith, one law and one king' no longer rang true. Martin Luther and his ideas were a success in many parts of Germany and, by the end of the sixteenth century, Protestantism had spread in some form or another to most corners of western Europe. Challenges to the teachings and structure of the Catholic Church had, in the past, come from men such as **Jan Hus**, the Bohemian reformer, but had always ended in failure. For Luther to be a success, the circumstances in Germany had to be favourable and, in that part of Europe, the Catholic Church cannot have been as healthy as in others. It is clear, therefore, that the Catholic Church continued to operate effectively in some areas, while in others it was stagnant and in need of reform.

THE POSITION OF THE CATHOLIC CHURCH IN SOCIETY

For the people of late medieval Europe, religion was of great importance. The Church played a central role in their lives, not just spiritually but also socially and economically. There were few non-believers in the practices and teachings of Catholicism. People generally believed that the Church provided all the right answers and that it was only through the Catholic Church that salvation could be attained. The people were linked to the Church in various ways.

- **Spiritually,** through the seven sacraments and the road to salvation. The seven sacraments (listed on page 5) were seen as a way of participating in the mystery of Christ through symbolic actions. Salvation was regarded as the deliverance from sin and admission into heaven

Jan Hus preaching. German engraving c.1850.

brought about by Christ. The fear of what awaited them after death was a very real one for early modern people, and the wish to attain salvation and enter heaven often guided their actions on earth.

- **Economically,** through taxation, the upkeep of the Church, and wills.
- **Socially**, through active participation in festivals and processions.
- **Pastorally,** through confession, penance and the cult of saints. Confession was a practice for early modern Catholics, during which the participant would acknowledge his sins to a priest. In order to makeup or atone for sins that had been committed, penance often had to be carried out. Penance might be regarded as a form of punishment for sins that had been committed and, depending on how serious the miscreant had been, the form of punishment varied from fasts and the carrying out of pilgrimages, to flogging and imprisonment. Yet absolution from one's sins was crucial to the laity, as many feared dying and suffering for unatoned sins. The cult of saints was the practice of worshipping the remains of saints. Saints were seen as being close to God and capable of communicating with God on our behalf: therefore, through the saints, divine

KEY PERSON

Jan Hus (1369–1415) was born in Husinec, which is now part of the Czech Republic. Having studied at Prague University, he soon became well known for his lectures and preaching on the theology and, in particular, the corrupt practices of the Catholic Church. In 1408, Hus defied a papal bull forbidding him to preach. Excommunication followed in 1411 and three years later he was called before the Council of Constance, where he denied the supremacy of the Pope and defended the teachings of the English reformer John Wyclif. He also refused to recant his many works, the most famous of which was entitled *De Ecclesia* and written in 1413. In 1415, Hus was burned at the stake, having been found guilty of heresy. This event sparked the Hussite wars in Bohemia in which supporters of the reformer fought for his views and principles. Hus is still revered in the Czech Republic today as a national icon, symbolised by his imposing statue in Prague's Old Town Square.

power could be accessed. Often, the laity picked out particular saints to worship, believing them to be capable of looking after their interests and protecting them from evil. Reformers such as Luther condemned the worshipping of saints because, for them, such practice blurred the unique status of Christ.

- **Educationally,** through the learning of doctrine. Doctrine can be regarded as a principle of religious belief. Such theology was taught to children and adults through church services, primers and catechisms. A catechism was a comprehensive account of Catholic doctrine, including the Apostles' Creed, Ten Commandments, Lord's Prayer and the Seven Sacraments. However, one should not forget that the Bible was in Latin, an edition known as the Vulgate which had been translated by St Jerome, and was therefore inaccessible to the majority of the laity.
- **Politically,** through the activities and policies of the local bishop.

The Sacraments

Unquestionably, the most important link between the Catholic Church and the people was the spiritual one. For the people of late medieval Europe, the path to salvation and heaven was found by following the teachings of the Church and this meant following the seven sacraments:

1 Baptism
2 Eucharist
3 Penance
4 Confirmation
5 Matrimony
6 Extreme Unction
7 Ordination

The Eucharist

Of these seven sacraments, it was the Mass, or celebration of the **Eucharist**, that was of crucial importance to Catholics. While a person was born only once, married once and died once, the hearing of Mass was a weekly, if not daily, event. By attending Mass, the people were recognising the visual embodiment of Christ and celebrating his ascension to heaven. The Catholic understanding of the Mass was based around transubstantiation. This idea was, and is, at the heart of Catholicism. In the Mass, the priest will bless or consecrate the bread and wine as part of the service. Through this process, Catholics believe that the consecrated elements of the bread and wine are transformed into the actual body and blood of Christ. One cannot underestimate how powerful this service was. The people truly believed that to celebrate the Mass was to witness a miracle and that it was only through attending Mass that salvation could be reached. It is unlikely that the ordinary people would understand the whispered Latin verse of the priest, yet they did understand the significance of the ritual.

Penance and sin

Also important to the belief of Catholics was, and is, the idea of sin. A sin is committing an offence against God. One could not receive the Eucharist in sin unless one repented (admitted guilt) and confessed one's sins. Repentance was therefore of great importance, especially because death was a major concern for the people of late medieval Europe (not surprising, given the regular outbreaks of war, plague and famine). Every Catholic wanted to be prepared for death, to have repented of sin before entering heaven. Catholics believed that to enter purgatory (the place in which souls were cleansed before entering heaven) would result in considerable suffering for the individual. This issue was a preoccupation of Catholics, and they had a number of strategies for dealing with it. However, the vast majority of the laity took communion (participated in the taking of bread and wine) only once a year – at Easter.

- Prayers and Masses for the dead were said in order to release loved ones from purgatory.
- Religious guilds existed in which lay people (non-priests) could say prayers and Masses for the dead.
- One's own time in purgatory might be reduced through the purchase of indulgences. Indulgences were pieces of parchment sold by the clergy and signed by the Pope offering a general pardon for sin and thereby releasing the faithful from purgatory. One can see why indulgences were a highly attractive proposition.

Participation

In general, religion in late medieval Europe was about participation and activity.

- **Feast days and saints' days.** Religious processions and pilgrimages to local shrines were popular, while feast days and saints' days attracted large crowds and were observed universally by the people. For example, Parisians celebrated the third of January as St Geneviève Day whereby the reliquary of St Geneviève was carried in procession to the cathedral. The church was a most important social centre for the people – a natural gathering point in what was predominantly a rural society.
- **The decoration of churches.** The loyalty and devotion of the people can be seen first through the building and decoration of churches. For example, the historian Susan Brigden tells us in *London and the Reformation* (Oxford 1989) that in London in 1500 there were over a hundred parish churches, a cathedral and 39 religious houses. The money to build and adorn such churches came from Londoners. This financial commitment came out of either a genuine devotion or merely from the hope that salvation might be attained through such good deeds. Yet the sheer number of **roods** surely illustrates a devotion to Christ, while the reliance upon saints throughout Europe indicates more than merely a **pragmatic** attachment to Catholicism. Indeed, images and paintings of saints were commonplace in the churches of Europe.
- **Devotion to saints.** There was a widespread belief that miracles were performed at the shrines of saints, and most people adopted a saint who they believed looked after them through curing illness or protecting crops. For example, St Bernard was deemed to look after beekeepers and wax melters, St Romanus of Rouen protected the inhabitants of that town from drowning, madness and poison, while St Apollonia was the one to call upon when suffering from toothache! In a period of great uncertainty, religion brought stability and solace. The most popular image was that of Our Lady, Mary, mother of Jesus. Throughout Europe, people paid for her image to beam down from windows or to inspire through statues. Even after death, men and women

KEY TERMS

Roods are replicas of the cross on which Jesus was crucified. Generally, roods were raised on a beam near the altar.

Pragmatic is when something is done for reasons of common sense.

would leave money to pay for candles to be lit before their favourite saint. Churchwardens' accounts from across Europe reveal the amount of money contributed by a community towards the upkeep, maintenance and expansion of churches during this period. Ornately gilded churches, glitteringly adorned with figures of saints, were in some ways testament to the devotion of the people.

- **Relics.** Most people believed in the power and importance of religious relics. Scepticism did not exist, and relics such as thorns from the crown of Christ or splinters from the True Cross were similarly bought or venerated (worshipped).
- **Financial payments.** Large amounts of money were left in wills to the Church and the laity also regularly paid taxation to the Church, often in the form of the tithe, which amounted to a tenth of all income and produce. Moreover, mortuary dues (money paid when people died), the Peter's Pence (a tax payable to the papacy) and the buying of indulgences represent other economic links between the laity and the Church. The taxes were regularly paid with little resentment.

All of the above suggest that, on the eve of the Reformation, the Catholic Church was in a strong and healthy state. Indeed, in many ways, it was the unifying bond of the community.

WHY WAS THE CATHOLIC CHURCH IN NEED OF REFORM?

Despite the strength of the Catholic Church explained above, there were aspects of the Church that had fallen into disrepair. This was noticeable across Europe, particularly in some of the German states. Corruption and abuse of position as a member of the Church among the higher ranks of the Catholic clergy was not uncommon. Such corruption existed at the very top.

The problems of the Papacy
Even the Pope in Rome hardly set a fine example. In 1500 the papacy was a powerful institution politically and

spiritually. The Pope was generally Italian and, although technically an elected position, through bribery it had become dominated by aristocratic Italian families such as the Medicis. Furthermore, a papal schism (split) in the fourteenth century (1309–77) had resulted in two Popes, one based in Avignon, the other in Rome. Although this was resolved by the beginning of the fifteenth century, successive Popes seemed to care more about wealth and prestige than spiritual leadership.

Top of most historians' lists of badly behaved popes comes Alexander VI (1431–1503). Formerly Rodrigo Borgia, Alexander VI was made a cardinal by his uncle, Pope Calixtus III, in 1455 before becoming Pope himself in 1492 on the death of Innocent VIII. It was widely recognised that Alexander owed his position to the widespread bribery of the College of Cardinals. Although Alexander started brightly by restoring order in Rome and challenging the authority of the Italian princes, he soon held a string of mistresses and fathered a number of illegitimate children, most of whom were looked after with clerical titles and income. In total, Alexander appointed 47 cardinals, including his teenage son Cesare. The luxury of the Alexandrian papal court knew no bounds while, as a patron of the arts, Alexander grew in stature, even commissioning Michelangelo to draw up plans for the rebuilding of St Peter's Basilica in Rome. Political manoeuvring and the furthering of his family were more important to Alexander than spiritual matters although, in 1498, he did oversee the burning of **Girolamo Savonarola**, who had been convicted of denying papal authority and preaching heretical doctrine. In 1503, Alexander died when he accidentally took poison at a dinner party hosted by Cardinal de Corneto. The poison had been intended for the host! Julius II (1503–13), the Warrior Pope, cared more about preserving his position in Europe amid aggression from France and the Empire, while his successor Leo X (1513–21) was obsessed with the building of the grandest church in Christendom, St Peter's Basilica in Rome.

During the sixteenth century, the Pope's position in central Italy became increasingly under threat from

KEY PERSON

Girolamo Savonarola (1452–98) was a religious and political reformer in Italy in the fifteenth century. He argued in favour of a moral reform of the Church. In Florence he insisted that gambling was forbidden and all costly clothes burned. However, Savonarola claimed he was a prophet and this led him into conflict with the Church. In 1498 he was executed, hanged and burned.

[handwritten margin notes: "evidence of nepotism", "politics more important than spirituality"]

Habsburg and Valois expansion. Therefore, in order to strengthen his defences the Pope looked to exploit the wealth of his subjects. Increased taxation and dispensations for marriage, as well as the sale of offices, all contributed to the wealth of the Curia (see page 32). Indeed, it was to the decentralised and easily exploitable German states that Rome looked to exploit most keenly.

Bishops and clergy

Furthermore, there was some evidence that such abuses filtered down into the ranks of the clergy. Complaints against archbishops, bishops and priests were various, such as:

- simony (the buying or selling of a benefice)
- nepotism (the securing of a benefice or post for one's family)
- pluralism (the holding of more than one benefice at the same time)
- absenteeism (the inability to be present in one's benefice in order to look after one's flock)
- clerical marriage (priests were not allowed to marry, but many did and had illegitimate children whom they might then maintain by providing them with positions in the Church)

Habsburg–Valois Conflict
Between the years 1521 and 1559, the royal houses of Habsburg and Valois were in conflict, with the chief protagonists in this struggle being Charles V, Holy Roman Emperor and Francis I, King of France. These two men were primarily fighting over dynastic claims and in particular the dominion of Italy. The significance of the conflict with regard to the Reformation was that, initially, Pope Leo X (1513–21) resented Habsburg intrusion into Italy and attempted to prevent Charles from becoming Emperor. In the long term, it took the attention of Charles V away from Germany, and Francis I, despite being Catholic, offered military and financial aid to the German Protestants in order to disadvantage Charles.

- illiteracy (ignorance of the Old and New Testaments and consequent inability to spiritually administer their flock).

The picture thus described is of a clergy that had lost its true sense of vocation and the ensuing resentment from the masses would seem inevitable. Yet, while such corruption did make the Church more vulnerable to attack in some areas, these abuses were exceptional and not necessarily widespread. Furthermore, given a certain set of circumstances, such low moral standards could certainly promote support for relatively radical reform.

WHO HAD PREVIOUSLY CHALLENGED THE AUTHORITY OF THE CHURCH?

Jan Hus — *Huss*

Few had attempted to challenge the one true faith because to do so might lead to a charge of heresy, and to be found guilty of such a crime would mean death, usually by fire. Yet some celebrated examples do exist. One such man was Jan Hus (1369–1415; see also page 4), who was burned alive on the order of the Pope because of his heretical views. Hus criticised the Catholic practice of communion, asserting that both the laity and the clergy should receive the bread and the wine, rather than the laity receiving only the bread. He also attacked the corrupt nature of the Church and the supreme authority of the Pope. Hus was summoned before Pope John XXIII at the Council of Constance in 1415 and, on refusing to recant his views, was found guilty of heresy. He was executed in 1415, as was his companion John of Prague the following year. Yet after his death, a small group of followers existed known as Hussites, who fought in the name of their reformer until the mid-seventeenth century.

John Wyclif — *Wycliffe!*

Hus himself owed much of his teaching to an Englishman by the name of John Wyclif (1329–84). He upheld the idea that the **Holy Scriptures** were the only valid source of truth and authority. Furthermore, he undermined the role of good works in salvation by emphasising the role of faith.

KEY TERM

The Holy Scriptures were the written word of God as outlined in the Old and New Testaments. For Christian humanists such as Erasmus, the problem with the Latin translations and the work of Church fathers such as Jerome, Origen and Augustine was that they were deemed to be inaccurate and, over time, had been misinterpreted. Humanists spent much time editing New Testaments, translating and writing biblical commentaries. For reformers such as Luther, the words and substance of the scriptures became the crux of Protestant calls for reform.

Moreover, he criticised the sale of indulgences. Followers of Wyclif became known as Lollards, and it was these men who undertook an early translation of the **Bible into English**. Wyclif managed to avoid the same fate as Hus. However, even in death he was thought to be dangerous by the Church. In 1428, his bones were dug up by the Catholic authorities and burned.

Both Hus and Wyclif ought to be regarded as important for a number of reasons. Many of their ideas were to reappear as part of Luther's criticism of the Catholic Church during the sixteenth century. It is interesting to note that neither Hus nor Wyclif gave birth to a popular or successful movement. This reveals something about the German environment in which Luther operated as well as about the man himself.

WHAT WAS THE IMPACT OF THE RENAISSANCE ON CATHOLICISM?

The Renaissance was important in the context of church reform because it encouraged a new intellectual outlook and a re-examination of accepted ideas. The Renaissance fostered Christian Humanism, an intellectual movement in which some important academics became preoccupied with studying, understanding and translating the original

KEY TERMS

Bible in English Although the Lollards undertook early translations of the Bible, the first translation from Greek into English to be published was by William Tyndale (1494–1536) in 1525. Tyndale's debt to Wyclif was enormous.

The Renaissance From the French meaning rebirth, the Renaissance is seen to centre around Italy, with the effects encompassing all of Europe. The period 1370–1527 is often deemed to be that in which literary and artistic talents such as Petrarch, Dante, Bruni and Boccaccio were allowed to flourish and a new wave of learning and thinking entered Europe. Whether such a period can actually be defined is a contentious issue, but the significance for the Reformation was that ancient, classical texts were re-evaluated and scripture re-translated. Also, Christian Humanism emerged from the literary and scholastic environment of the Renaissance.

Painting of Desiderius Erasmus by Hans Holbein the Younger, etched by Lefort.

scriptures. Through this study of the original scriptures, it was believed that authoritative interpretations could be made and old mistranslations put right. Furthermore, this fresh outlook also involved discussion of a reform of the practices of the clergy. Four men in particular are worth noting in any discussion on humanism.

- **Desiderius Erasmus (c.1466–1536).** The foremost humanist in Europe was Desiderius Erasmus, from Rotterdam. He talked about a restoration, by which he meant an improvement of Christianity through the translation and interpretation of sacred texts. Erasmus himself translated the New Testament into Greek in 1516 and into Latin in 1519. Although one would never label Erasmus as a revolutionary, there is little doubt that such translations paved the way for later German editions overseen by Luther. Moreover, moral criticism of the corrupt and worldly clergy from Erasmus in his *Praise of Folly* (1509) further weakened the Church. Erasmus, it must be stressed, was not like Hus or Wyclif. He did not propose a split from the Catholic Church and he was not opposing its fundamental doctrines. He was putting forward ideas to make people better Christians and to reform the Catholic Church from within. Indeed Erasmus demonstrated his conservatism when, after initially supporting the radical Luther, he then condemned him in his work of 1524 entitled *On the Freedom of the Will*. Luther responded with *De Servo Arbitro*, or *On the Bondage of the Will*, and the split was sealed.
- **Johannes Reuchlin (1455–1522)** was a German humanist trained in the law and noted for his exposition and understanding of Hebrew texts. His *De Arte Cabalistica* (1517) was seen as an important contribution to unravelling the ancient Jewish tradition of mystic interpretation of the Bible. Reuchlin was, until his death, a Roman Catholic, but the controversy caused by his work in Rome made him an intellectual forerunner for Luther and in some ways paved the way for the criticisms made by the Wittenberg reformer.
- **Ulrich von Hutten (1488–1523).** In Germany, humanists such as Ulrich von Hutten were to include a patriotic tone in their writings. He and others made

clear their nationalist resentment of a foreign Pope as is shown in von Hutten's work entitled *Vadiscus*. It can be argued that von Hutten laid the foundations for Luther's challenge. Von Hutten even pledged military support for Luther in the early years of the movement, thus suggesting a more radical stance than Erasmus.

- **Thomas More (1478–1535)**. Thomas More should be judged as another of these great academics who had little wish to break with the Catholic Church. Instead, More argued for change from within the existing structures of the Church. More's *Utopia* (1516) has been hailed as one of the great works of the period, and in it we can find criticisms of European society and the Church. Yet the happy island state that More learned of in *Utopia*, was not Protestantism. Like Erasmus, he ultimately showed his conservatism when, upon hearing of Luther's challenge, he wrote the *Assertio Septem Sacramentorum* (Assertion of the Seven Sacraments) which was a stark condemnation of the views of Luther. More became a victim of **Henry VIII's Great Matter** when, in 1535, he was executed for refusing to endorse the annulment of Henry's marriage to Catherine of Aragon and, in particular, the right of parliament to carry out such a procedure.

In some ways, these men – and perhaps especially Erasmus – were therefore academic forerunners to Luther, especially in their endorsement of original scripture. Yet they were no threat to the Catholic Church; indeed they were very much a part of it.

CONCLUSION

There is little evidence to suggest that the Church was becoming more unstable as it entered the sixteenth century.

- Corruption and abuse among the clergy had been occurring for centuries and again it should be stressed that such behaviour was generally isolated and localised.
- In many ways, abuses among the higher echelons of the clergy were accepted as the norm.

KEY TERM

Henry VIII's Great Matter
In 1527 Henry VIII declared that his marriage to Catherine of Aragon was invalid. Instead, he wanted to marry Anne Boleyn. In 1532 More resigned as the King's Chancellor because he disapproved of Henry's decision to ignore the view of the Pope and divorce Catherine. In 1534 Henry declared himself Head of the Church of England. He demanded that all his leading subjects should take an oath of supremacy. All who refused, such as More, were liable to execution.

- Yet while adherence to the Church remained the one means of grace and salvation, it was vulnerable.
- The Church rather set itself on a pedestal by claiming to be the sole interpreter of the Bible and the issue of papal supremacy implied a special and superior status. Such authority was accepted by the masses in 1500. Yet just over half a century later the Holy Roman Empire would house two faiths.
- The challenge from Luther was a relatively radical one, which paid scant respect to existing Church laws and belief. Clearly the German environment, and in particular the anti-clerical sentiment which existed there, aided his struggle.

SUMMARY QUESTIONS

1 What evidence exists to tell us that the Catholic Church was in a healthy state in 1500?

2 What were the criticisms being made of the Catholic Church in 1500?

3 Which people had previously challenged the authority of the Church?

4 How radical were the ideas of the Christian Humanists?

CHAPTER 2

What was the nature of Lutheranism?

LUTHER CHRONOLOGY

1483	Born the son of a copper miner in Eisleben.
1493–1500	Attends school in Mansfeld, Magdeburg and Eisenach.
1501	Matriculates at the University of Erfurt where he reads liberal arts in preparation for a career in the law.
1505	Struck by a bolt of lightning during a storm; a reputedly life-changing experience as Luther now commits himself to God, proclaiming to St Anne that he will become a monk.
1506	Takes the monastic vows of the Augustinian order.
1510	Visits Rome on behalf of the Augustinian friars and returns appalled with the worldly and material nature of the papacy.
1512	Receives a doctorate of theology from the University of Wittenberg.
1514	Begins preaching at the church in Wittenberg.
1513–8	Lectures on Romans, Galatians and Hebrews to the students of Wittenberg, from which his views on the role of faith in salvation become clearer.
1517	Posts his Ninety-Five Theses on indulgences to the door of the castle church in Wittenberg.
1518	With the succession of Holy Roman Emperor Maximilian I under discussion, Frederick the Wise of Saxony gains Luther a hearing with Cardinal Cajetan in Augsburg rather than the papally preferred venue of Rome.
1519	Leipzig disputation with Johannes Eck.
1520	Leo X issues the bull *Exsurge Domine*, which provisionally excommunicates Luther from the Catholic Church.
1520	Luther has his three great works published, defining his doctrine and beliefs. The *Address to the Christian Nobility of the German Nation*,

The Liberty of a Christian Man and *The Babylonish Captivity of the Church* are regarded as Luther's three most important works.

1521	Condemned by the Emperor Charles V at the Diet of Worms and, by the resulting edict, he is proclaimed a heretic and his books are to be burned.
1521	Resides in Wartburg Castle where he translates the New Testament into German. Published in 1522, Luther continually revised it until his death. The translation of a readable and commonly accessible New Testament in the vernacular was crucially important to Lutheranism.
1521	The radical Andreas Carlstadt takes control in Wittenberg, celebrating the first evangelical communion and carrying out attacks on Catholic statues and images.
1522	Returns to Wittenberg and restores order with his Invocavit sermons.
1523	Prepares a baptismal service and numerous hymns in German.
1525	Marries Katherine Von Bora, a former nun whom he had helped to escape from Nimbschen Convent with eleven others in 1523.
1525	Peasants' Revolt erupts in southern Germany. Luther condemns the disorder in his tract *Against the murdering thieving hordes of the peasants.*
1525	Split with Erasmus complete after Luther writes *De Servo Arbitro.*
1526	*German Mass* completed.
1529	Large and small catechisms published in German, allowing the common man access to Lutheran doctrine.
1529	Marburg Colloquy with Zwingli results in failure to agree over the Eucharist.
1536	Wittenberg Concord overseen by Bucer brings compromise between north and south Germany over the Eucharist.
1537	*Schmalkalden Articles* offer an overview of Lutheran theology and justify resistance to the emperor.
1546	Dies in Eisleben.

MARTIN LUTHER: THE EARLY YEARS

In order to understand Martin Luther's challenge to the beliefs and rituals of Catholic Europe, one must recognise that Luther himself did not set out to lead a breakaway movement from the Catholic Church. Indeed, he had chosen to join the Augustinian religious order at Erfurt in 1505 as a novice monk and thereafter enter the priesthood in 1507. As a monk, he had decided to devote his life to God through prayer and contemplation. However, in 1510, Luther travelled to Rome, a visit that opened his eyes to certain aspects of the Catholic Church. When he returned to Germany he was transferred to the monastery at Wittenberg and made a professor at the university. There is little doubt that Luther was a troubled man during these early years in Wittenberg. Luther's problem was questioning the nature of Christianity, along with his relationship and understanding of God. However, at Wittenberg, he met **Johannes von Staupitz**, an important member of the Augustinian order who helped him overcome his doubts and torment. The questions he asked went to the heart of the Catholic faith.

The path to salvation

Luther felt an overwhelming sense of guilt and inadequacy in trying to meet the demands of a perfect God. In short, Luther was highly sceptical of the Catholic Church's view that man could make himself acceptable to God through his own efforts. Good works alone seemed inadequate to Luther as the means of setting an individual on the road to salvation. This obviously contradicted the teaching of the Catholic Church at the time. In attempting to discover the secrets of his religion, Luther turned to the Bible. From 1513, he undertook a study of the scriptures under the watchful eye of Johannes von Staupitz. He lectured at the university on sections of the Bible: in 1513 he lectured on the Psalms; in 1515 his lectures were on St Paul's Epistle to the Romans. Later, Romans 1:17 would lead Luther to recognise that God's justice did not consist of a demand but rather it was a gift given by God to humans and received through faith alone. Reading the Bible, preparing his lectures and discussing issues with von Staupitz led Luther to certain important conclusions.

KEY PERSON

Johannes von Staupitz (1460–1525) was an Augustinian adviser and ecclesiastical superior of Luther in his capacity as Dean of the Theological Faculty of Wittenberg. Luther turned to him for spiritual help and guidance during his troubled period over the role of faith in salvation. Von Staupitz found it difficult to comprehend Luther's doubts but did his best to emphasise to him the positive aspects of God's grace. Later, Von Staupitz freed Luther from his Augustinian vows as the Reformation took hold.

Faith

For Luther, the most important revelation that came out of his studying the Bible was the importance of faith. The Epistles of St Paul revealed the key to his problems. The scriptures stated that God would extend mercy and salvation to all those who identified through faith with Jesus Christ. Luther came to believe that man never ceased to be a sinner before God. Christ was the only man who satisfied the demands of God. Therefore, in order for man to be saved and enter heaven, he had to put his trust in faith alone. The line in the Bible in the gospel according to St Paul read 'the just shall live by faith' and from now on this idea was to form the crux of Luther's doctrine. The implications for the Catholic Church were serious.

Luther's ideas on faith and salvation undermined the role of good works, as they now became a sign of salvation rather than a cause. Furthermore, **indulgences** and the idea of purgatory were also under threat from a doctrine that stated that salvation was freely offered by God to all people.

In 1515, these radical teachings were causing a stir among the students and professors of Wittenberg University, and Luther showed no signs of letting up on his beliefs.

THE INDULGENCES AFFAIR

Luther and indulgences

It is hardly surprising that Luther should take issue with the sale of indulgences, given his views on salvation. His condemnation of indulgences was based on the following objections:

- Luther saw pieces of **parchment**, authorised by Rome, which lessened time in purgatory, as corrupt and insulting to God. For a man who based his teachings on the scriptures, such methods were mercenary.
- The sale of indulgences confirmed Luther's criticisms of the papacy as a worldly institution, which exploited the common man.
- Luther's objections were hardly likely to fall on deaf ears

KEY TERMS

Indulgences In the Catholic Church, the belief was that the Pope could issue a pardon for sins committed on earth that would mean that an individual would not have to serve time in purgatory for his or her sins. These pardons were called indulgences.

Parchment A parchment is a stiff, flat skin of an animal used as a writing surface.

IOHANNES TETZELIUS, PIRNENSIS
MISNICUS, MONACHUS ORDINIS SANCTI DOMINICI
FRANCOFURTI AD ODERAM, PRAECO, FORNICARIUS ET
NUNDINATOR, BULLARUM PAPALIUM
INDULGENTIARUM Anno 1517
Denatus d. 7 Augusti Anno 1519.

Johann Tetzel's *Sale of Indulgences* (contemporary handbill).

Pope Leo X (1475–1521)
The son of Lorenzo de Medici, Leo was groomed for papal office from his days at university in Pisa. On becoming Pope in 1513 he sought to exclude foreign influences from Italy, while courting important monarchs such as Francis I. Indeed, Leo favoured either Francis or Frederick of Saxony succeeding Maximilian as Holy Roman Emperor, rather than another Habsburg in the form of Charles. However, the Imperial electors voted otherwise and Leo shortly had to turn his attentions to Luther. Notably in 1517, Leo X had to appoint 31 new cardinals after a plot to poison him was uncovered!

Johann Tetzel (1465–1519) Having studied at Leipzig, Tetzel quickly rose through the clerical ranks, being named inquisitor for Poland and later Saxony. In 1517, he preached indulgences for St Peter's in Juterborg and Zerbst, near Wittenberg, while serving the Archbishop of Mainz. Thus Tetzel came into contact with Luther and the indulgences affair sparked into life.

given the anti-clerical sentiments of the masses, fuelled by the news that the profits from the sale of the indulgences would go towards the building of St Peter's Basilica in Rome.

Actually, much of the money went to Albert of Brandenburg, Prince-Archbishop of Mainz, so that he could repay the money he had spent bribing important clergymen and princes to elect him. This deal was approved of by **Pope Leo X**. Such justifications merely spurred Luther on to denounce indulgences with greater venom. The arrival in Wittenberg in 1517 of **Johann Tetzel**, a Dominican indulgence-selling monk, prompted action from Luther.

The Ninety-Five Theses

In autumn 1517, Luther read a copy of the *Instructio Summaria*, issued by the Archbishop of Mainz to guide indulgence sellers such as Tetzel. Indulgences were portrayed as a convenient way of absolving one's sins and reconciling oneself with God. Tetzel himself preached to the people that in these letters of indulgence all the ministries of Christ's passion are engraved and etched, while preachers were also encouraged to associate the coin falling into the money chest with the soul moving from purgatory into heaven. The rhyming couplet,

As soon as coin in coffer rings
The soul from purgatory springs,

illustrated this for the laity. Luther had already preached against the errors of indulgence selling and written a letter of complaint to the Archbishop of Mainz, so, when he decided to prompt an academic disputation on the matter, the content of the theses was already formulated in his mind. In the traditional fashion, Luther nailed his Ninety-Five Theses to the castle church door in October 1517, inviting those interested to discuss the matter. The theses outlined the way in which indulgences did not contribute to a good Christian life and indeed obscured the word of God. Below are some examples from the theses, which were originally written in Latin. Traditionally, the posting of Luther's Ninety-Five Theses is seen as the beginning of the German Reformation. Of course, Luther had no idea that a popular movement would emerge from such criticisms.

Thesis 4

Hence as long as hatred of self remains the penalty of sin remains, that is, until we enter the kingdom of heaven.

Thesis 7

God never remits guilt to anyone without at the same time humbling him in total submission to the priest, his representative.

Commentary: Here, Luther is asserting that man never ceases to be a sinner and cannot make himself perfect in the eyes of God. One should not try to take the easy way out through indulgence buying, but rather show true repentance by accepting punishment.

Thesis 21

Hence those preachers of Indulgences are wrong when they say that a man is absolved and saved from every penalty by the Pope's Indulgences.

Thesis 27

It is mere human talk to preach that the soul flies out of purgatory immediately the money clinks in the collection box.

Commentary: Here, Luther is asserting that the Church has no real power over the souls of the dead in purgatory, while also referring to the aforementioned jingle.

Thesis 32

All those who believe themselves certain of salvation because of letters of pardon will be eternally damned together with their teachers.

Thesis 38

Yet the Pope's remission and dispensation are in no way to be despised for as already said they proclaim the divine remission.

Commentary: Luther here states that those lulled into believing that buying indulgences will bring salvation will themselves be damned. Also, he interestingly notes that indulgences are not to be totally dismissed as they do bring some solace to the weak and insecure.

Thesis 50

Christians should be taught that if the Pope knew the exactions of the preachers of Indulgences he would rather have the basilica of St Peter reduced to ashes than built with the skin, flesh and bones of his sheep.

Commentary: This shows a harsh and provocative attack on the corrupt practices of indulgence sellers.

Thesis 62

The true treasure of the Church is the holy Gospel of the glory and the grace of God.

Commentary: Luther extols the virtue of preaching the Gospel, the true word of God, which is in danger of being obscured by indulgences.

Thesis 86

Since the Pope's wealth is larger than that of the crassest Crassi of our time, why does he not build this one basilica of St Peter with his own money, rather than with that of his faithful poor?

Commentary: Although the theses were not meant for widespread circulation, one wonders if Luther knew that they might be circulated in German, for here is a point aimed directly at the common man, reinforcing widespread anti-clerical sentiments.

Thesis 94

Christians should be exhorted to seek earnestly to follow Christ their Head through penalties, deaths and hells.

Commentary: Luther brings the theses to a close with a reiteration of the merits of true faith and repentance in attaining salvation.

The impact of the Ninety-Five Theses. Luther's purpose was not to rouse the people into revolt, but to prompt an academic debate on the essence of salvation and to make people aware that men such as the Pope and the Archbishop of Mainz were endangering souls. Yet Luther was bound to bring attention to himself and, by the end of 1517, printed editions of his theses had reached Leipzig and Nuremberg. Shortly thereafter, Luther became famous throughout Germany. The angry reaction of the Archbishop and Tetzel merely helped to escalate the affair. Tetzel remarked that Luther would shortly be in flames

while, in Frankfurt in January 1518, Dr Conrad Koch drew up retaliatory theses on behalf of Tetzel, repudiating the claims made by Luther. The undergraduates at Wittenberg burned 800 copies of the counter-theses. Meanwhile, Luther travelled to Heidelberg for a meeting of the **Augustinian order**, where he defended his theology for the first time outside Wittenberg. It became clear that the Catholic Church was going to have to deal with Luther.

The Catholic reaction

The response of Leo X. The new-found notoriety Luther had attained through his attack on indulgences was not entirely unintentional. After all, Luther had gone public by pinning the Ninety-Five Theses to the castle church door. Furthermore, he had not greatly objected to the public circulation of his ideas. Yet the controversy was still very much an academic, scholarly one and was treated as such by the Catholic authorities. Pope Leo X ordered Luther to travel to Rome in order to answer for his opinions and

> ### KEY TERM
>
> **Augustinian order** In 587 St Augustine was sent to England to reform the Church of England. He set up a monastery in Canterbury and was chosen to be the first archbishop. The order that followed the rules of St Augustine is known as the Augustinians.

KEY PEOPLE

Cardinal Cajetan (1469–1534) became a cardinal in 1517, having served as the official Dominican representative in Rome. Although Luther thought him as fit to deal with his case as an ass was to play the harp, Cajetan was actually able and wrote several tracts defending the papacy and various elements of Catholic doctrine. Neither was he a blinded bigot, even suggesting to Pope Clement VII in 1530 that communion in both kinds and clerical marriage should be conceded to the Protestants as a sign of compromise.

Johannes Eck (1486–1543) was Luther's main opponent. The turning point in his career as a theologian was the appearance of Luther, and other Protestant reformers. Apart from being an active proponent of Catholic ideas in debate, he wrote a number of works attacking Luther, Zwingli and other reformers. Most important of his works was *Arguments against Luther and Other Enemies of the Church*, first published in 1525.

beliefs, an invitation he declined. Instead, the Pope sent an Italian representative, **Cardinal Cajetan**, to Germany. His task was to make Luther aware of the grave errors in his beliefs. Further to that he was to make clear the danger of expressing such opinions. In the eyes of the Catholic Church, Luther was implicitly denying papal supremacy and he had to be publicly reprimanded and made to see the error of his ways. Yet Rome was about to encounter, for the first time, the stubborn and courageous nature of Martin Luther.

Meeting at Augsburg, 1518. Cardinal Cajetan did meet Luther in October 1518 at Augsburg, but he was far from successful in making the latter alter his opinions or recant. Cajetan's aim was to persuade Luther to take back his views on indulgences. However, Luther held firm, stating that unless his views could be proven to be incorrect through scripture, he would not change them. This meeting had two important consequences:

- First, it succeeded in increasing the notoriety/popularity of Luther.
- Second, it strengthened the stand-off position that had already developed between Rome and Luther.

In Catholic eyes, the supreme authority in matters of religion was the Pope and Luther needed to be made aware of this. In Luther's eyes, the Church was flawed in its interpretation of the scriptures, and as long as he did not bow to the inevitable pressure that would be exerted upon him, the stage was set for further and more serious confrontation.

Luther and Johannes Eck

In June 1519, Luther was involved in a set piece disputation (a debate) with **Johannes Eck** (1486–1543), a theologian from the University of Ingolstadt in Bavaria. The two met at Leipzig in order to debate the issue of papal primacy and the route to salvation. Luther was in the public spotlight against one of the finest minds in Europe. Eck is generally seen to have triumphed in this dispute because he successfully identified Luther with the fifteenth-century heretic Jan Hus. In fact, Luther himself admitted that he shared many of the views of the Bohemian reformer. Yet Luther maintained that if such views had the authority of scripture, then Hus was correct, just as he was. In short, how could such men be heretics if they were supported by the word of God? Luther was now putting himself into a very dangerous position. After all, Hus had been burned for his views.

Luther's increasing publicity was worrying for the papacy. Academic debates had not moved Luther; the time to increase the pressure had come. Eck journeyed to Rome soon after Leipzig and helped draft the papal bull *Exsurge Domine*, which condemned 41 propositions drawn from Luther's work and threatened Luther with excommunication.

In June 1520, Leo X issued the bull *Exsurge Domine*, and both Eck and Girolamo Alexander were commissioned as special **nuncios** to publish the bull in the empire. *Exsurge Domine* opened with the phrase, 'Arise O Lord … a wild boar seeks to destroy the vineyard'. The boar was of course Luther and the papal bull gave Luther 60 days to **recant**, or face excommunication. Luther's response was to write, *Adversus Execrabilem Antichristi Bullam*, which proclaimed the Pope to be Antichrist and defiantly stated that 'this thing shall neither console nor frighten me'. Most of northern and central Germany rejected the bull, and calls by Eck to burn the works of Luther were rejected in Cologne. On 3 January 1521, Luther was officially excommunicated by the bull *Decet Romanum Pontificem*. He could no longer attend communion and receive the Eucharist. He was now a rebel and an outcast. In typically defiant and almost showmanlike style, **Luther burned the papal bull** and prepared to stand firm. More importantly, he started to lay down his teachings on paper.

THE THEOLOGY OF LUTHER

The year 1520 was an extremely busy one for Luther, as he had 24 works published. This was the year in which Luther explained his theology (views about God) in writing.

Three works in particular are of great importance:

- *Address to the Christian Nobility of the German Nation*, August 1520.
- *The Babylonish Captivity of the Church*, October 1520.
- *The Liberty of a Christian Man*, November 1520.

In these three works Luther developed his vision of Christianity:

- He clarified what he believed a true Christian was, how a true Christian should lead a Christian life and the manner in which a true Christian should worship.
- In *Address to the Christian Nobility of the German Nation*, Luther appealed to a patriotic audience and the elite of society. He called upon the princes to undertake and oversee reform. Luther believed that they were the ones who had been given authority by God to rule, and it was their duty to usher in reform of the Church. Therefore, even at this early stage, signs of Luther's conservatism were evident, in that he was calling upon the ruling elites to introduce change from above.

Most importantly, in 1520 Luther proceeded to set out his theological programme, which revolved around the following ideas:

- **Justification by faith alone** was the crux of Luther's theology. Luther argued that man was always a sinner in the eyes of God and could not secure salvation through good deeds on earth. Instead, man had to put his trust in God and seek salvation through true faith and the unselfish love which resulted. Good works may still be seen as a sign that the individual was saved, but were now totally undermined as a cause of salvation. This point of doctrine was outlined in *The Liberty of a Christian Man*, and typified Luther's belief that he had unearthed, in the Epistles of St Paul, a crucial piece of theology that had escaped the Catholic Church for centuries.
- **The position of the clergy.** Luther argued that the laity should receive both the bread and the wine during communion. The doctrine of communion in both kinds

meant that the laity would receive both the bread and the wine rather than just the bread as they had done up until now in the Catholic Mass. He was challenging the spiritual superiority of the clergy, which allowed them both bread and wine, and in doing so he was questioning the hierarchical structure of the Catholic Church.

- Moreover, linked to the priesthood of all believers and the idea that priests were little different from other people, was Luther's authorisation of clerical marriage. Indeed, in 1525, Luther himself married Katherine Von Bora, an ex-nun with whom he had six children.

- **The sacraments.** There were only three sacraments which Luther recognised as having scriptural authority: the Eucharist, baptism and penance. Later, Luther would deny the sacramental status of penance as well. Moreover, Luther denounced the central Catholic doctrine of transubstantiation, stating that no miracle took place during the sacrament of the altar. However, Luther did affirm the bodily transformation of the bread and the wine and he was certainly not as radical as later reformers such as **Huldrych Zwingli**, who totally denied the real presence of Christ in the Eucharist. Yet, by denying that this sacrament was a sacrifice, he was undermining a very important part of Catholic worship.

- **The priesthood of all believers** was also based upon the principle of scriptural authority (*sola scriptura*), and was outlined in the treatise entitled *The Babylonish Captivity of the Church*. In this work, Luther argued that the sacrament of ordination had no foundation in the Gospel. Just like his attack on the clerical superiority in receiving both bread and wine during communion, Luther targeted faith as being the important issue. To Luther, an ordination rite was no symbol of superiority; rather, true faith was all-important. Luther was not exactly saying that everyone was a priest if they had faith. Instead he argued that, for priests, spiritual guidance from reading the scriptures was important, and that each was to serve his neighbour as Christ had served humanity. The significance of his views was that he was undermining the established Catholic clergy by stating that their ordination into the priesthood did not necessarily put them in a superior position to the laity. This challenge to the Catholic hierarchy was deliberately provocative.

KEY PERSON

Huldrych Zwingli (1484–1531) was a Swiss reformer who studied at Bern, Vienna and Basle, before entering the priesthood in Glarus. In 1526, after a personal meeting with Erasmus, he became convinced that doctrine and worship had to be guided by scripture, and his own beliefs became more evangelical in nature. In 1518, he took up the post of people's priest in Zurich where, over the next decade, he led a reform movement. In 1525, the Reformation in Zurich seemed complete with the abolition of the Mass. The views of Zwingli concerning *sola scriptura* and the Eucharist are laid out in his 67 articles of 1523. Most notably, Zwingli disagreed with Luther over the nature of the elements in the Eucharist, with Zwingli asserting that the bread and the wine remained just that during communion. Such disagreement prevented unity between the two reform movements, characterised by the unsuccessful Colloquy of Marburg in 1529. Zwingli died in 1531 on the battlefield during the Second Kappel War.

- **Attack on the papacy.** Throughout his works, Luther also attacked the Church over other issues. These included papal primacy, papal ignorance of the scriptures, the wealth of the Catholic Church and superstition.

Luther's audience. After 1520, Luther cleverly began to adapt his message to suit a wider audience. He knew that criticism of papal taxation would not fall on deaf ears in a Germany resentful of seeing their hard-earned money disappear over the Alps to a foreign figurehead they had never seen before. Moreover, communion in both kinds and the priesthood of all believers, if described simply, were messages of equality and freedom, which could appeal to peasants resentful of powerful landlords. Luther wrote countless pamphlets or *flugschriften*, which were eagerly received by the literate populace and read aloud to the rest. To say, therefore, that Luther's doctrine had little effect on the common man would be false, although just how much the laity actually understood is questionable. Many took from Luther's message what they wanted and ignored the rest.

THE EMPEROR INTERVENES

The Diet at Worms. In April 1521, Luther was summoned before His Imperial Majesty Charles V, **Holy Roman Emperor** and the most powerful man in Christendom. Indeed, Luther was fortunate to be given a hearing, as it would have been entirely appropriate for the emperor merely to endorse the bull of excommunication issued by Leo X. Luther could have been arrested without a further hearing and charged with heresy. Yet, due to the pressure placed upon him by the German princes, the young emperor decided to allow Luther a final chance to recant his views. Luther was even allowed to travel to and from Worms, where the **Imperial Diet** was to meet, under a promise of safe conduct. Jan Hus had travelled to the Council of Constance under such an agreement in 1415, yet he had not escaped the flames. Luther was in real danger and he knew it.

The Holy Roman Empire.

Map showing:
- Boundary of the Holy Roman Empire
- Lübeck, Hamburg, Bremen, BRANDENBURG, Brunswick, Magdeburg, Berlin
- SPANISH NETHERLANDS, Aachen, Cologne, SAXONY, R. Elbe, R. Oder, SILESIA
- R. Rhine, Trier, Mainz, Frankfurt, Prague, BOHEMIA
- PALATINATE, Regensburg
- Strasburg, WURTTEMBERG, BAVARIA, R. Danube
- R. Rhône, LORRAINE, Augsburg, Munich, Vienna
- R. Loire, Berne, SWISS CONFEDERATION
- SAVOY, Milan, R. Danube
- R. Rhône, Turin, Genoa

Luther's appearance at Worms displays the courage of the man, but he probably stood defiant safe in the knowledge that Charles V was unlikely to act rashly and provoke the wrath of the princes, or even popular unrest. One must remember that Charles had relied upon the votes of the Seven Electors of the Holy Roman Empire and to risk antagonising them after only two years of office would have been foolhardy. On 18 April 1521, Luther stood before Charles for the first and only time:

- Luther acknowledged his own writings and refused to recant, for to do so would not be right, as this very retraction would again bring about a state of affairs where 'tyranny and impiety would rule and rage among the people of God'.
- Luther maintained his fundamental doctrines and the stand-off which had begun at Augsburg remained in place.

The imperial response was a predictable one. Charles V denounced Luther as a heretic and ordered the bull *Exsurge Domine* to be enacted immediately. The Edict of Worms stated that Luther's writings were to be burned and citizens of the empire were forbidden to house, feed or protect the heretic Luther. Both Church and emperor had now outlawed Luther, but Charles did stand by his word and allowed Luther to leave Worms unharmed.

THE ROLE PLAYED BY FREDERICK THE WISE

The extent of Frederick's influence

An important factor in explaining the rise to prominence of Luther was the protection of his political lord, the **Elector Frederick of Saxony**. Frederick had supported Luther upon hearing of his stand against indulgences, not so much because he agreed with Luther's theological and moral stance, but because he wanted to protect the academic reputation of the University of Wittenberg, as well as preserve his own territories from external influence and intervention – that is, intervention from Charles V.

Frederick III of Saxony (1463–1525) was Elector of Saxony from 1486 until his death, during which time he sought to curb the power of Charles V over the state of Saxony. Frederick helped Luther by preventing the reformer's extradition to Rome in 1518, as well as protecting him throughout and offering advice, most of which was relayed through his secretary and friend of Luther, Spalatin. Not only had Charles relied upon Frederick in 1519 for his imperial vote, but he also owed him money, with debts dating back to 1497. It may have been for these reasons that Frederick was not sent the Edict of Worms and Charles did not take more forceful action. His nickname was Frederick the Wise.

Frederick the Wise, Elector of Saxony, by Cranach the Elder.

The importance of Frederick was that he was one of the seven imperial electors and, as such, he held the right to vote on who would become emperor. Indeed, Charles had relied upon Frederick's vote in 1519, when he succeeded his grandfather Maximilian I. Therefore, if Charles were to establish his authority in the Empire, then he would need the support of men such as Frederick.

Therefore, the Elector of Saxony was a powerful ally for Luther. Just how powerful was demonstrated in the wake of the Edict of Worms. On his way back to Wittenberg after the Diet of 1521, Luther was kidnapped by men under the authority of Frederick and taken for his own safety to Wartburg Castle. The young Charles V made no attempt to seek him out or have him arrested. The potential power of the princes in the Empire had been clearly demonstrated. Luther spent his time at Wartburg translating the New Testament into German, thereby opening up the scriptures to the people. While he was safe, the movement grew around him, and it became clear that Luther would have to return to Wittenberg to oversee its development.

CONCLUSION

In many ways the Diet of Worms represents a watershed mark in the career of Martin Luther:

- The secular condemnation by the emperor and princes at the Diet of Worms of 1521, following the clerical denouncement by the Pope of the previous year, put Luther in a new light. No longer was this an individual pursuing a theological debate. Luther was now a condemned heretic around whom a popular movement was developing. Indeed, there are signs even before Worms that Luther was becoming a popular figure throughout Germany. In February, the papal **legate**, Aleander, reported that the whole of Germany was in revolt and that 'nine out of ten people cry Luther and the rest death to the Roman **Curia**'. Moreover, Aleander promptly ordered a burning of Luther's books in Cologne. Yet he was one of the few to actively carry out the Edict of Worms.

KEY TERMS

Legate A legate was a papal ambassador whose job it was to relate the views and policies of the Pope to foreign courts.

The Curia was the papal civil service or administrative unit.

There was little doubt that, by 1521, the message of Luther had found receptive ground in his homeland.

SUMMARY QUESTIONS

1 How did Luther's teachings differ from those of the Catholic Church?

2 How did Luther's attack on indulgences undermine the Catholic Church?

3 What was the significance of Luther's meetings with Cajetan and Eck?

4 How vulnerable was Luther at Worms in 1521?

CHAPTER 3

What were the reasons for the success of Lutheranism?

EARLY SETBACKS

Andreas Carlstadt

Amid the remarkable success of Lutheranism during the period 1521–5, there were also some serious moments of crisis. When Luther returned to Wittenberg in 1522 after his period of captivity in Wartburg Castle he faced a local populace influenced by **Andreas Carlstadt** (1486–1541), a colleague of Luther at the University of Wittenberg. In Luther's absence, Carlstadt had assumed the lead role in church government at the expense of **Philip Melanchthon** and **Gabriel Zwilling**. Luther was concerned that Carlstadt was proposing more radical and quicker change than he had envisaged:

- Among Carlstadt's ideas was the need to cleanse churches immediately of images and altars, using violence if necessary.
- Already, Carlstadt had taken a fifteen-year-old wife, named Anna von Mochau, and he encouraged clerical marriage, including monks, to proceed rapidly.
- Moreover, Carlstadt and his followers had welcomed the extremist group named the **Zwickau Prophets** into the town, and it was becoming clear that the word of God was being used as a vehicle for radical change and that order was in danger of being lost.
- Carlstadt differed from Luther over the central moment in the Mass. Whereas Luther argued that the bread and wine should still be offered up as a mark of reverence, Carlstadt disagreed, believing that there should be no sign of sacrifice.
- Carlstadt had encouraged the smashing of statues of saints, images of God and religious pictures in churches, a process known as iconoclasm.

KEY PEOPLE

Carlstadt, Melanchthon and **Zwilling** were all supporters of Luther.

KEY TERM

Zwickau Prophets were from nearby Bohemia. Among their claims were the suggestions that they were in close communication with God, had no need of the Bible and that the ungodly should be slaughtered!

Between 1521 and 1522, Wittenberg became a hotbed of religious change. It was not unknown for priests and monks to marry nuns from the local convent! Some priests conducted religious services in their own clothes. Notably, the friar Zwilling celebrated the Lord's Supper wearing a beret with a feather in it! Luther returned to Wittenberg in December 1521. He put on his Augustinian robes and delivered eight sermons denouncing Carlstadt and his pace of change, as well as the use of violence in promoting reform. Luther had demonstrated his conservatism for all to see.

The Peasants' Revolt, 1525

Background to the revolt. The Lutheran message undoubtedly made an impact in the countryside among the peasant population. Luther's message was initially a flexible one and an accessible one, as woodcuts and rhyming passages, along with Lutheran missionaries from the cities, opened up the scriptures to the rural community. While at Worms in 1521, Luther had awoken one morning to find the sign of revolutionary peasants, the Bundschuh (clog) painted on doors throughout the town in support of his stance. Yet there was a danger that Luther's message might be misinterpreted, or reinterpreted, if too much flexibility and freedom was allowed.

Although the peasants essentially owed allegiance to their lord and paid dues and taxes to him, rural communities were run by village communes. These communes had significant powers in overseeing local affairs and the reforms proposed by Luther gave them an opportunity to take greater control over the Church and challenge the existing feudal order. Rising prices and pressure on land, combined with discontent over taxation, provided the social and economic stimulus.

Despite Luther's attack on superstition, peasant society was deeply conservative. In astrological predictions, the year 1524 had been identified as a year of rebellion; in 1523 there were no less than 51 tracts speculating on the subject. This prophecy increased tension in the countryside considerably.

Throughout Germany, attempts to arrest Lutheran ministers, as part of the enforcement of the Edict of Worms, often led to a peasant reaction in defence of Lutheranism. It is not hard to see how Luther's message of the priesthood of all believers and the attack on clerical hierarchy could be adapted to mirror the landlord/peasant relationship.

The Twelve Articles. In 1525, the peasants of Germany, in particular those in the south, rose up in rebellion against the ruling classes. A list of grievances entitled *The Twelve Articles of Memmingen* was drawn up by one band of peasants complaining of overbearing lords and hefty taxation. Luther's message was incorporated into the complaints, and the authority of scripture was often (falsely) used to reinforce peasant demands and complaints. One should not underestimate the scale of the revolt, with over 100,000 peasants involved. Noble estates and monasteries were targeted by the peasants; by the end of the war, around 270 castles and 52 cloisters had been destroyed. However, there was little co-ordination or leadership involved in their efforts.

Thomas Müntzer. One leader of note was Thomas Müntzer (see page 67) in Thuringia. He was an extremist who urged his followers to use violence to root out the ungodly in society in order to prepare for the millennium. Yet, once the law-enforcing Swabian League was put into action, the peasants stood no chance and they were ruthlessly crushed at a battle near Frankenhausen in 1525. Thousands of peasants were executed and Müntzer was decapitated for his part in the uprising. Luther was horrified at the events and the way in which the word of God was being used to justify the lawlessness and violence of the peasants. Luther hurriedly wrote a tract entitled *Against the murdering, thieving hordes of the peasants* (1525) in which he condemned the actions of the peasantry. Published just after the peasants had been crushed, it reflected badly on Luther, as the work seemed to endorse the slaughter. Luther had not meant this, but he was adamant that open rebellion was unacceptable.

Significance of these early setbacks

The actions of Andreas Carlstadt and then the Peasants' Revolt were significant for three reasons:

- They confirmed Luther's belief that reform had to be initiated and guided from above; that is, from the city magistrates and princes, as he had outlined in his treatise *Address to the Christian Nobility of the German Nation* (1520).
- These events also emphasised for Luther the dangers of allowing the laity to read the scriptures and interpret the word of God for themselves. Preachers and teachers were necessary in the localities in order to guide and instruct.
- Carlstadt and the peasants demonstrated that Lutheranism could not be the all-embracing movement it had threatened to become during the period 1520–5. The peasants were largely alienated by the events of 1525. As it became clear that Lutheranism was developing as a conservative movement under the guidance of the princes, extremist splinter groups emerged such as the Anabaptists (see page 66).

By 1525, Lutheranism had developed into a popular movement. What had begun merely as a theological, academic debate had exploded into a powerful protest, which found support in the cities and the countryside. The implications of this movement were profound as, by 1555, Germany would have two faiths recognised by the

Religious Peace of Augsburg. In short, the whole structure and order of religious life in Germany would change as a result of the success of Lutheranism. In order to explain the success of Luther's challenge one must look not only at the role of the individual himself, but also at the environment in which he operated. Crucial to the success of the movement were the following factors:

- The nature and accessibility of Luther's message was of central importance to the success of the movement.
- Luther was a brave and courageous man.
- Circumstances unquestionably favoured Luther, as he was able to exploit widespread German anti-clericalism and appeal to patriotic sentiment.
- The protection that Luther received from some princes such as Frederick the Wise and later, and more importantly, Philip of Hesse allowed the movement to develop in the face of a troubled and inexperienced Holy Roman Emperor.
- Princely support became more organised and official in the form of leagues established in 1526 at Torgau and in 1531 at Schmalkalden to defend Lutheranism.

Therefore, Lutheranism saw two phases during the period leading up to 1555.

- From 1520 to 1529, Lutheranism emerged quickly and spectacularly as a mass movement.
- From 1530 to 1555, the movement became increasingly shaped by the actions of the princes and one could argue that, in their hands, Lutheranism was consolidated and politicised.

HOW DID LUTHERANISM BECOME A POPULAR MOVEMENT BY 1525?

The role of individuals
Martin Luther. Clearly one cannot discuss the success of Lutheranism without assessing the importance of its founder, Martin Luther. As we have already seen, Luther initiated the challenge to the existing Catholic Church through his condemnation of its practices and doctrine. Moreover, Luther displayed great courage in maintaining

his position and standing firm in the face of the accusations and threats made by Cardinal Cajetan, John Eck, the papacy and the Holy Roman Emperor, Charles V. Furthermore, Luther's energy and creativity resulted in a mass of literature and it would be fair to say that, by 1521, Luther had laid down his theological agenda on paper, epitomised by the three great works of 1520 (see page 27).

There were other individuals who undertook the task of spreading the ideas of reform. In north Germany, **Johannes Bugenhagen** carried out much work in organising reform. Yet, Luther was not just one reformer among many, he was exceptional. It was Luther who drove the Reformation in the early years, writing and printing with unbelievable vigour. It was Luther to whom the people looked as a figurehead and talisman. While his influence may have diminished after 1530, Luther remained a crucial figure, for it was he who maintained the authority of pure gospel amid Catholic threats, and it was he who was increasingly seen as a German hero by the common man. Luther very skilfully tapped into the anti-clericalism that existed in Germany and deliberately adapted the Lutheran message to fit varying audiences and circumstances.

Philip Melanchthon (1497–1560). It is important to also consider the role of Luther's young protégé, Philip Melanchthon. It was he who wrote the first systematic and pure work of the new faith in 1521, entitled *Loci Communes*. Bearing in mind that Luther was effectively in captivity in Wartburg Castle between 1521 and 1522, other scholarly individuals were required to make an impact. Melanchthon was the most important, not only in laying out an organised explanation of the new faith, but also in trying to restrict the radical tendencies of others, such as Andreas Carlstadt, who wanted to accelerate the rate of reform and change. Notably, it was Melanchthon who, in 1530, drew up the *Confession of Augsburg* – the Lutheran statement of belief.

The flexibility of Luther's message

Furthermore, the publication of a **German New Testament** in 1522 was a major contribution to the early

Melanchthon preaching. Engraving after Lucas Cranach the Younger c.1560.

Reformation in Germany. This was because the scriptures were now in the mother tongue and therefore accessible to the literate section of the population. The message of justification by faith alone and the primacy of the scriptures had been set out by Luther and, by 1521, this message was gradually spreading from the cities into the countryside, through the mediums of **printing** and **preaching**. Perhaps most importantly during these early years of success (1521–5), the movement was broad ranging, in both its appeal and its support. It must be stressed that this was a deliberate ploy by Luther. The

Lutheran message was a flexible one and Luther readily adapted it to suit differing audiences. In some ways the people of Germany took from Luther's message what they wanted:

- The so-called nurseries of the Reformation were the cities, such as Nuremberg, where a disproportionately literate population could be found. This was a population more likely to understand the finer points of Luther's theology, and identify with it. Therefore, while the artisan in Augsburg might not understand the intricacies of the priesthood of all believers, he would identify with the anti-clerical message that went alongside it.
- Yet, perhaps as much as 90 per cent of the German population lived and worked in the countryside and, if the movement was to become truly popular, it would have to spread from its original home in the cities. The fact that it did, especially in the south, was partly due to the flexibility of the message. Moreover, in the countryside, local village leaders saw the Reformation as a chance to establish greater control over the parish church at the expense of the existing clergy. Yet there is

Luther preaching. German woodcut.

obviously a danger in allowing such flexibility, in that Luther's message could be misread and adopted for more radical purposes, something Luther did not want. However, as we have seen, this is generally what happened in 1525 with the Peasants' Revolt.

The situation in the Holy Roman Empire

One really ought not to talk of Germany during this period, but rather a Holy Roman Empire made up of over 400 small and politically autonomous states. Yet there is little doubt that the circumstances that existed in the Empire meant that Luther's message was guaranteed to find fertile ground among the people of the German states.

- The anti-clericalism that existed in Germany has already been discussed (see pages 8–10 and Chapter 2), but it needs to be stressed that opposition to Rome and discontent with the Catholic Church gave Luther the opportunity to set out his programme of reform and espouse the pure gospel.
- Moreover, the people of Germany were ready to identify with one of their own. Luther became a figure of German nationalism, a patriotic icon around whom the people could put forward their grievances with the Church. Events such as the disputation with Eck in 1519 or the Diet of Worms in 1521 merely enhanced Luther's image as an honest, courageous and worthy German battling against the odds to overcome the powerful and corrupt forces of the papacy.
- The common man could identify with Luther, rather than a foreign figurehead who resided hundreds of miles away. Luther rode on the back of this patriotic sentiment, writing specifically to the nobility of the German nation in 1520 (see page 27).
- Furthermore, the publication of a New Testament in German in 1522 had an enormous impact, selling out within three months and going through another 300 editions before Luther's death in 1546. Not only does this illustrate his popularity but also the readiness of the people to read the scriptures in their own language. Moreover, the Emperor's fear of executing such a popular national figure perhaps ensured Luther's survival in 1521 at Worms.

The German states

The German states were also well suited to receiving Luther's message:

- The Holy Roman Empire contained a relatively large number of cities. Whereas England had only one city of any size, namely London (with a population of around 100,000), the Holy Roman Empire had several. Nuremberg, Augsburg and Hamburg all housed between 50,000 and 100,000 people, while Bremen, Lübeck and Magdeburg had between 20,000 and 50,000 inhabitants during the sixteenth century.
- These cities not only provided a large and disproportionately literate population, among whom the message could be spread, but they also contained universities and printing presses where the word of God could be translated and printed. Lutheran preachers spread the word among the majority who were illiterate. Woodcuts, images and illustrations were also produced to accompany the written word and to disseminate the message among as many as possible (see pages 40 and 41).
- One should also not forget that cities such as Hamburg lay on internal and external trade routes, which allowed the message to spread widely among the merchant classes.

It was in the cities that the German Reformation took off between 1521 and 1525, with the people providing the pressure on the local authority to embrace reform.

Charles V (1500–58)

Charles V is perhaps the most important political figure in sixteenth-century Europe. His inheritance was massive. On the death of his father, Philip I, he took over the Netherlands, Luxemburg and Franche-Comté while, on the death of his grandfather Ferdinand of Aragon, he became King of Castile and Aragon and ruler of Navarre, Sicily and Naples. The death of his other grandfather, Maximilian, in 1519, opened the door for Austrian Habsburg lands and the Holy Roman Empire.

Charles was only nineteen-years-old when he was elected emperor in 1519. He was inexperienced and needed the

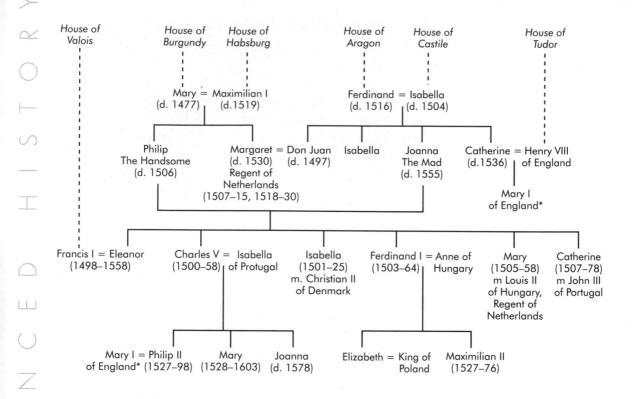

The Habsburg family tree, showing links to royal houses.

House of Valois — **House of Burgundy** — **House of Habsburg** — **House of Aragon** — **House of Castile** — **House of Tudor**

Mary (d. 1477) = Maximilian I (d.1519)

Ferdinand (d. 1516) = Isabella (d. 1504)

Philip The Handsome (d. 1506)

Margaret (d. 1530) Regent of Netherlands (1507–15, 1518–30) = Don Juan (d. 1497)

Isabella

Joanna The Mad (d. 1555)

Catherine (d.1536) = Henry VIII of England

Mary I of England*

Francis I = Eleanor (1498–1558)

Charles V (1500–58) = Isabella of Protugal

Isabella (1501–25) m. Christian II of Denmark

Ferdinand I (1503–64) = Anne of Hungary

Mary (1505–58) m Louis II of Hungary, Regent of Netherlands

Catherine (1507–78) m John III of Portugal

Mary I = Philip II of England* (1527–98)

Mary (1528–1603)

Joanna (d. 1578)

Elizabeth = King of Poland

Maximilian II (1527–76)

support of the princes, a dependence that ensured Luther's survival at Worms in 1521. Had Charles been able to remain in the Empire and devote more energy to the task of unifying the Church, he might well, with time, have succeeded. Yet, the longer he was absent, the stronger and more accepted Lutheranism became. The vast nature of Charles V's inheritance and Empire meant that he was unable to give full attention to the spread of Lutheranism in Germany. Indeed, during that crucial period of 1522–9, Charles was not present in Germany. The Emperor's preoccupation with the French threat in northern Italy and rebellions in Castile and Valencia in Spain allowed Lutheranism to gain a foothold so that, when in 1543 Charles entered Germany for only the third time, he was confronted with an irresolvable problem.

Charles delegated responsibility for the day-to-day running of the Empire to his brother, Ferdinand, yet too often the imperial policy was one of playing for time in order to allow Charles to direct his attentions and finances

Painting of Charles V, Emperor from 1519, by Jan van Orley.

elsewhere. For example, in 1526 at the Diet of Speyer (see pages 51–2), the decision was made to allow princes to decide upon the implementation of the Edict of Worms. The result was that those in favour of reform, such as Hesse, did not enforce it. Charles would have liked to have been more decisive, yet this was not possible because of the threat of the **Ottoman Empire** in the Mediterranean and the continuing battle with the French king, Francis I, over Italy.

Protection and support

The nobility. We have already seen the role of Frederick the Wise in supporting and protecting Luther during and after the Diet of Worms, although one would hardly call him a committed Lutheran. Few other princes leapt to Luther's defence during the early years of the Reformation, primarily because they did not initially want to identify themselves with such a radical movement. The success of Lutheranism was by no means guaranteed and, while Luther specifically appealed to the German nobility in

KEY TERM

Ottoman Empire The most successful and powerful state in Europe between 1450 and 1600. Its navy controlled the Mediterranean, its army was formidable. The leader of the Empire between 1520 and 1566 was Suliman the Magnificent. In 1529, he laid siege to the Habsburg capital Vienna, and in 1540, large parts of Hungary were annexed, thus proving that the Ottoman Empire was a constant threat to Charles.

1520 for support in reforming the Church, they remained aloof, preferring to see how Lutheranism would develop. In some senses, it was just too risky for the princes to back Luther during the early years.

The Imperial Knights. Luther himself was wary of armed support, as he maintained a strictly **pacifist** approach to reform at this stage. Luther's position was illustrated in 1521 when he refused the support of the Imperial Knights, an independent group of minor noblemen whose forefathers had been extremely influential during the Middle Ages, but whose influence had now waned. They did, however, possess military backing and were ready to raise arms in Luther's name against the Emperor and some German princes. In particular, one of their humanist leaders, Ulrich von Hutten, recognised the national appeal of Luther. Luther declined their assistance on two counts:

Pacifist A pacifist is someone who believes in peace and is therefore opposed to violence or use of arms as a means of settling disputes.

- He already had the influential support of Frederick the Wise.
- There was little to be gained by such violent methods at this stage.

Luther was proved correct in his judgement when, in 1523, another of the knights' leaders, Franz von Sickingen, was defeated by a group of local princes after he had attempted to seize the Archbishopric of Trier.

As Lutheranism became a stronger and accepted force from the mid-1520s onwards, some princes gradually changed their views and moved to support Luther. The first to do so was Albrecht of Hohenzollern, Grand Master of the Teutonic Knights, followed in 1526 by Philip of Hesse. Indeed, in 1526, a grouping of Lutheran princes emerged in the form of the League of Torgau, led by the Elector of Saxony and Hesse and designed to prevent the implementation of the Edict of Worms. When the princes became Lutheran, they turned their subjects over to the new faith, either because they themselves were committed believers in Luther's message or because of public pressure in favour of Luther. The material benefits of secularising Church lands also appealed to the German princes. Generally, the role of the princes was far more important after 1530, when the movement was largely in their hands and became more conservative in nature as a result.

WHAT DID IT MEAN FOR A TOWN TO BECOME LUTHERAN?

The towns and cities, as we have seen, were areas of spectacular success for Lutheranism, illustrated by the fact that, by 1550, a total of 50 out of the 65 imperial cities were adhering to the new faith. The decision to adopt Lutheranism generally came from the town council, yet often they were under severe pressure from the local populace to do so. By 1525, Erfurt, Magdeburg, Nuremberg and Bremen had embraced reform. Augsburg and Strasburg joined them in 1534. However, to abandon Catholicism was one thing, but to set up a new church structure was quite another and often proved problematical. Yet, generally, adopting Lutheranism meant a number of changes:

- The Catholic Mass was abolished and replaced by a German Mass or communion rite. The *Deutsche Messe* written by Luther, was published in 1526 and acted as the new reformed liturgy.
- Communion in both kinds was introduced.
- Altars and images were removed from churches.
- Baptismal and marital services were performed in German.
- Clerical marriage was permitted.
- A reformed catechism was introduced, through which the laity could be educated in the new faith. Luther published two catechisms in German in 1529.
- The clergy were re-educated in the new faith. Initially itinerant (travelling from place to place) Lutheran preachers had a large role to play in the preaching of the gospel. Men such as Andreas Osiander in Nuremberg were very important.
- The territorial prince was responsible for the uniform practice of religion. The ruler of each state would appoint visitors whose job it was to investigate worship in the parishes of the state and ensure that good practice was being observed.

The adoption of a new church structure was always going to be a lengthy and difficult process. Luther soon became aware, through the radicalism of Carlstadt in 1522 and the Peasants' Revolt of 1525, that the scriptures could not be left entirely in the hands of the people, and city magistrates and princes were urged to guide reform. It was up to men such as Melanchthon and Bugenhagen to establish a church structure that incorporated a trained ministry.

The reaction of Erasmus and the humanists

After 1525, the movement became more political and consolidation was in the hands of the princes. However, while describing the movement as conservative, one must not forget just how radical and revolutionary the initial challenge had been. Indeed, it was too radical for the great humanist Desiderius Erasmus. In 1524, he wrote against Luther for the first time in his work. *On the Freedom of the Will*, which specifically denounced Luther's doctrine of justification by faith alone. The ageing Erasmus had stayed loyal to his Catholic roots, which was not surprising given the status and wealth he had accumulated over the years. He had too much to lose by supporting Luther. The humanistic criticism and scriptural enquiry of Erasmus had once inspired Luther, and their split in 1525, sealed with Luther's retaliatory *On the Bondage of the Will*, was symbolic of how far Lutheranism had come. Younger humanists with less to lose tended to remain with Luther.

SUMMARY QUESTIONS

1 Why did the ideas of Luther appeal to the German populace?

2 How did the composition of the Holy Roman Empire aid the spread of Luther's message?

3 What was the most important factor in explaining Luther's success?

4 How did Luther adapt his message to suit different groups of people?

CHAPTER 4

How did Lutheranism consolidate and expand?

THE POLITICAL CONTEXT OF THE GERMAN REFORMATION

Introduction

It became apparent to Luther after the Peasants' Revolt of 1525 that the guidance and direction for reform had to come from the princes. In Luther's mind the princes owed their position of authority to God, and as a result it was their duty to oversee reform. Moreover, if the Lutheran movement was going to survive and expand in the years after the Edict of Worms of 1521 (see page 31), then it was going to need the support and protection of the princes.

The attitude of the princes

Although the princes were initially unwilling to commit themselves totally to the Lutheran cause, generally for fear that the movement might be short lived and collapse, as time passed more and more territorial lords threw their lot in with Luther. Princes embraced reform for a variety of reasons:

- Some princes were committed Lutherans, such as Philip of Hesse or John of Saxony.
- Some were pressurised by the local populace into adopting Lutheranism, such as the Archbishop of Mainz at Erfurt.
- Others wished greater freedom from Habsburg authority, such as the Palatinate or Anhalt Dessau.
- Moreover, the material benefits of reform could be great as the secularisation of church lands brought greater revenue and power, as shown by Albrecht of Hohenzollern, the first prince to support Luther.

Princely support was therefore crucial to the survival and consolidation of Lutheranism. After 1525, princely support became more committed and organised, in the form of military, defensive leagues, the most significant being the Schmalkaldic League. By 1555, over half of Germany was ruled by Lutheran princes.

The search for unity, 1530–55

From 1530 onwards it became clear that warfare was inevitable, as two armed camps had emerged, based on religion. The main aim of imperial policy was to find a solution that would restore religious unity. In 1541, Charles V still believed, 24 years after the Luther affair began, that a doctrinal compromise between Catholicism and Protestantism could be found. In retrospect, this was naïve, as Lutheranism had laid down strong foundations and compromise over religious doctrine was unlikely. Charles V's absence from the Empire lessened his chances of success and, although on his return a military victory was achieved over the Lutherans at Mühlberg in 1547, the fact that he was unable to enforce Catholicism upon the populace demonstrates that Lutheranism was embedded within Germany. The Religious Peace of Augsburg in 1555 declared what many had felt inevitable for some time, but which had been unthinkable for Charles V – a bi-confessional Germany.

The implementation of the Edict of Worms.
The initial rapid expansion of Lutheranism in the cities and then in the countryside took place in the face of the Edict of Worms, which had outlawed Luther and banned his books. The fact is that the Edict was largely ignored by those cities and states intent on reform. The relative political autonomy of the princes and the cities, especially in the south of Germany, allowed Lutheranism to be adopted in safety. Charles V left behind a regency council after the Diet of Worms, but it was entirely ineffective and lacked the resources and the will to enforce the Edict. Towns such as Hamburg and Nuremberg abandoned the Catholic Mass and printed Luther's work openly, and without any real fear of retribution. After all, **Ferdinand of Austria** could not risk major civil unrest.

The lack of central control is clearly demonstrated by the three Imperial Diets, which met at Nuremberg between

KEY PERSON

Ferdinand of Austria was Charles V's younger brother and had been entrusted by Charles with the ruling of the Empire while Charles was in conflict with France. In 1522, Ferdinand had made an alliance with the two Dukes of Bavaria and the Bishop of Southern Germany in the hope of checking the spread of Lutheranism. The two brothers fell out in 1550 over who would succeed Ferdinand as Emperor. Charles proposed his son Philip, while Ferdinand promoted his son Maximilian. A compromise was reached, whereby Philip would succeed and thereafter the succession would alternate between the two branches. Ultimately, the princes were so annoyed by this private settlement that enough pressure was brought to bear on Philip to renounce his succession and Maximilian II took over in 1564.

1521 and 1524. A strict enforcement of imperial policy was impossible given the political power and independence of the princes. Without any central control to enforce the Edict of Worms, those princes who wished to root out Lutheranism and defend Catholicism were forced to do so on their own initiative. In 1524, the regency council was dissolved and the Catholic League of Regensburg was established under the authority of Ferdinand of Austria and the Duke of Bavaria, along with the spiritual backing of the south German bishops. Further evidence that the Catholic princes were willing to take matters into their own hands came in 1525, when the League of Dessau was created, headed by Duke George of Saxony. These organised groupings demonstrated that imperial policy would have to be implemented through force, and this was unlikely to happen given that this period witnessed the greatest expansion of Lutheranism. However, the fact that warfare did not commence until the mid-1540s demonstrates that Charles believed a peaceful solution to the religious division in Germany could be found. Indeed, Charles urged Ferdinand to negotiate with the papacy and call a General Council of the Church at which the situation in Germany could be discussed and, hopefully, defused through reform from within the Catholic Church.

Torgau and Speyer. In response, the Lutherans, led by Philip of Hesse, formed the rival League of Torgau in 1526, which was intent on ensuring that the Edict of Worms would not be enforced. Therefore, one can see a pattern emerging, which would hold for the next 20 years:

- Imperial policy was to find a compromise and restore unity.
- Yet, in the meantime, the lack of central imperial control and the absence of Charles V meant that the spread of Lutheranism could not be stopped.

Partly as a consequence, two rival groupings emerged and, as time passed and compromise became increasingly unlikely, war appeared inevitable. However, while the possibility of negotiations existed, Charles instructed Ferdinand to play for time. The Diet of Speyer in 1526 was a good example of this tactic. It was most conciliatory towards the emerging religion. The Diet declared the following:

- The Edict of Worms would be implemented as each thought right before God and his imperial majesty. In short, the princes could interpret the edict as they wished. Effectively, toleration had been granted and this declaration unquestionably gave Lutheranism the time and space necessary to consolidate its early gains.
- Church lands that had already been taken were to remain secularised.

Over the next three years, Lutheranism developed in a secure environment and further towns embraced reform, while more princes joined the likes of Albrecht of Hohenzollern and Philip of Hesse in the defence of Lutheranism.

Charles acts against Lutheranism

Given this temporary period of toleration, one might have expected greater organisation of Lutherans on military lines, yet Luther himself condemned armed resistance to a higher authority and most princes heeded his decree. Charles V was determined to overturn the Speyer legislation as quickly as he could and in 1529 he was in a position to do so; his quarrel with France had been settled by the Treaty of Cambrai. The second Diet of Speyer in 1529 saw the 1526 decree overturned, declaring that no more church land was to be secularised and the Edict of Worms was once more to be enforced strictly. Certainly this was a setback for the Lutheran princes and it demonstrated Charles V's ultimate commitment to one faith within the Empire, through negotiation or force. Yet, for Charles, the problem remained of how to enforce the Edict of Worms effectively. The aggressive declaration at Speyer in 1529 was met with an aggressive response from the Lutheran princes.

- Six princes and fourteen imperial cities made a collective stand against Charles V, issuing a Protestation against the 1529 legislation.
- The commitment of the Lutheran princes to the word of God was increasing and the stakes in this religious conflict were being raised. The protesters, from whom we derive the term Protestant, were openly challenging imperial authority, answering to God not Emperor.

The Diet of Augsburg, 1530. Nevertheless, Charles V appeared to be in a strong position in 1529. The Recess of 1526 had been rescinded while, in 1529, the Lutheran movement appeared to be showing signs of division: Luther denounced the Swiss reformer Huldrych Zwingli at the **Marburg Colloquy**, thereby ensuring a split within Protestantism. Moreover, the situation in eastern Europe and Italy appeared favourable for Charles V – so much so that the Emperor was able to turn his attentions fully to Germany in 1530. Charles travelled to the Diet of Augsburg with the aim of restoring unity within the Church, while also enlisting German aid for the ongoing struggle against the Ottoman Turk. Furthermore, Charles wanted princely approval for his brother Ferdinand's nomination to be King of the Romans, a position that would make Ferdinand the heir to the imperial throne. Therefore, in some ways, we can still note a conflict of interests for Charles at the Diet of Augsburg. Perhaps it was the need to court the German princes that led to Charles seeking a theological compromise. Theologians from both the Catholic and Protestant camps were invited to attend the Diet yet, realistically, there was little chance of reaching a compromise.

Confession of Augsburg. The Lutheran **Confession of Augsburg** was a moderate declaration of the new faith, a deliberately mild document drawn up by Melanchthon in the hope that it might be accepted. Yet, even this watered-down definition of Lutheranism still omitted the central Catholic beliefs of purgatory and transubstantiation, while denying papal supremacy. The lesson was clear: it did not matter how such a confession was worded or how mild it might be doctrinally, such beliefs were too radical for Charles V. No middle ground could be found on issues such as the Eucharist, and Charles should have recognised this after Augsburg. The Emperor did of course reject the confession presented to him by seven Lutheran princes, and shortly afterwards an unrealistic deadline of April 1531 was set for the return of all Lutherans to the Catholic Church.

The Schmalkaldic League, 1530–43. Charles' aggressive decree after Augsburg, combined with the stated re-affirmation of the Edict of Worms, prompted a predictable response from the Lutheran princes. In 1531, a princely alliance was formed at the town of Schmalkalden, led by Philip of Hesse and including the princes of Anhalt, Mansfeld, Braunschweig–Lüneburg and the Elector of Saxony. Eleven imperial cities also joined the league in 1531, including Strasburg, Ulm and Bremen. The importance of the Schmalkaldic League should not be underestimated:

- The League represented the most formal and organised opposition to imperial power up to this point. Not only were its members agreeing to help each other should they be attacked on account of the word of God and the doctrine of the Gospel, they were also renouncing their membership from all imperial institutions.
- For the first time, a group of princes was operating outside the recognised political structure of the Empire, and the theory that the emperor could not be opposed by force was being reversed.
- Even Luther insisted that, if a war broke out, those who opposed murderers and bloodthirsty papists would be acting in self-defence against an unjust force.

Protestant interests now had a powerful backing and the empire was clearly divided into two armed camps.

Peace of Nuremberg, 1532. Unsurprisingly, the Schmalkaldic League received backing from the French king, Francis I, eager to exploit divisions within the Empire and hinder the progress of Charles V. Moreover, Charles' continuing problem with the Ottoman Empire meant that he had to once more compromise his position in 1532. The Religious Peace of Nuremberg gained men and money for the fight against the Ottoman leader Suleiman, but conceded toleration to the Protestants until a General Council could be called at which the split could be discussed and, in Charles' eyes, healed. This toleration, combined with the fact that, between 1533 and 1542, Charles was not in Germany, once more allowed Lutheranism the chance to lay down firm foundations under the protection of the League. The expansion was not like that of the 1520s – dramatic, urban and revolutionary

Luther declared himself thoroughly displeased with such a shallow and conciliatory outline of Lutheranism.

– but gradual and encompassing large expanses of territory. The power of the League was clearly demonstrated in 1534, when Duke Ulrich was restored to his Duchy of Württemberg at the expense of the Habsburgs. Aided by French financial backing, the League forced Ferdinand and Charles to recognise Duke Ulrich as the rightful ruler, and such a victory displayed the strength of the League to other princes, who now felt confident enough to join up.

The long road to war. The Lutheran cause received a further boost in 1536, when the **Wittenberg Concord** ensured unity among the German Protestant states. At the heart of this unity was agreement about the nature of the Eucharist. The inevitable road towards war was also further underlined in 1537, when the **Schmalkalden Articles** justified resistance to the emperor in the cause of the word of God. The 1530s ended, however, without such a war taking place. The preoccupation of Charles with Francis I and Suleiman, combined with the strength of the League and the inability of the papacy to summon a General Council of the Church, meant that Protestantism continued to expand. Indeed, in 1541 at Regensburg Charles appeared to be repeating the same mistakes of the Diet of Augsburg in 1530. However, the events at Regensberg seemed to make matters more final. Once more, theologians were invited to attempt to reach a doctrinal compromise. Once more, such a compromise was impossible. Religious matters had developed too far and opinions were so polarised over issues such as papal supremacy and transubstantiation that finding a middle ground was out of the question. Charles was forced to concede what, in retrospect, had been evident since 1530: that military means were the only remaining solution.

Charles re-entered Germany in 1543 for only the third time in his imperial life. A year previously, the last remaining Catholic prince in the north, Duke Henry of Brunswick–Wolfenbüttel, had been driven out by the League. Therefore, potential support for Charles in the north of Germany was thin on the ground. Charles would remain in Germany for twelve years and depart a broken and defeated man, leaving behind him an empire in which Catholic and Protestant states co-existed.

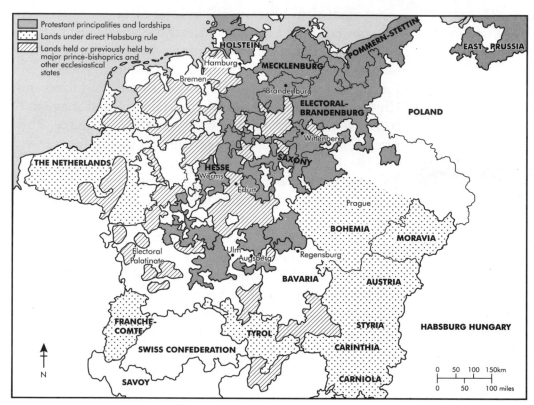

Key
- Protestant principalities and lordships
- Lands under direct Habsburg rule
- Lands held or previously held by major prince-bishoprics and other ecclesiastical states

German principalities on the eve of the Schmalkaldic War, c.1547.

Divide and Rule 1543–8

Opportunity for the Habsburgs. On Charles' return, however, the situation was looking brighter for a Habsburg re-conquest of Lutheran gains. Indeed, there were signs that the Schmalkaldic League was beginning to crack:

- In 1541, **Philip of Hesse** was exposed as a bigamist and, worse still, Luther had given him the authority to marry again. Hesse had to plead for his life before the emperor, as bigamy was a capital crime punishable by death. He was pardoned but, as a political force, he was ruined.
- Furthermore, the defeat of France in 1544 removed foreign aid to the League and freed Charles to concentrate on Germany. The Turkish threat in Hungary came to nothing and, with papal help assured, Charles could set about breaking the League.
- With war on the horizon and the diplomatic position favouring Charles, Martin Luther died on 18 February 1546, aged 63. By this time, he had become rather impatient and cantankerous, scornful of those who did

not agree with his doctrinal position. Perhaps such stubbornness prevented a unification between various strands of Protestantism, yet one cannot underestimate his significant achievements.

The Battle of Mühlberg, 1547. Charles continued to clear the way for war, luring Maurice of Saxony and the Margrave of Brandenburg to his side through bribery and promises of power. Such young princes who had no grounding in the origins of the religious schism were easily won over, yet their defection was a clear sign that the powerful League of the 1530s had disappeared. The crucial battle came in 1547 at Mühlberg in Saxony. Despite having a numerical advantage (the Schmalkaldic force numbered 80,000 in comparison to the imperial force of 56,000), the Schmalkaldic army was no match for the experienced and well-equipped Spanish troops of Charles V. The result was a crushing victory for Charles V. John Frederick, the Elector of Saxony, was captured and, as promised, his lands were turned over to Maurice. The League crumbled and it appeared that all of Germany was in the hands of Charles V.

The Diet of Augsburg, 1547–8. Yet such a victory as that at Mühlberg did not mean that Charles could impose his Catholic will upon the populace. Lutheranism was too strong at grass-roots level for any Catholic decree to be observed. Many German towns had been worshipping in a Lutheran manner for the past 20 years. The resulting Diet of Augsburg in 1547–8 proved this point:

• Charles laid out plans for a strengthening of central government, something which the princes never enjoyed hearing, as their privileges and traditions would be compromised.
• An Augsburg Interim (1548) was drawn up which gave few concessions to Lutheranism and effectively formed a Catholic statement of belief, which was to be observed by all cities and states in the Empire. The Interim was to be imperial law until a General Council of the Church decided upon matters of doctrine.

The Augsburg Interim in some ways was a chance lost by

Charles to invoke a realistic and workable peace settlement upon the population of Germany. Yet one would have expected little else from such a man as set in his ways as Charles V. He had strived all his imperial life for unity based upon the doctrine of Catholicism. He was unlikely to abandon such principles now, especially after such a great military victory. Yet the Interim was largely ignored by the princes and city magistrates of the Empire, while Charles did not have the means to enforce it.

The Religious Peace of Augsburg, 1555. Charles' attempts to enforce a moderate re-Catholicisation of the Empire were only successful in those areas where his army was present. Moreover, the Habsburg family itself was showing signs of strain as Charles sought to promote his son Philip to the imperial throne after his death at the expense of Ferdinand. Such disunity was seized upon by the young Maurice of Saxony, newly-entitled Elector of Saxony. Charles' policy of divide and rule backfired as the maverick young Maurice led a sizeable army south, boosted by French aid in a bid to free his father-in-law Philip of Hesse and gain the city of Magdeburg, thereby consolidating his electoral title. This revolt forced Charles to flee into Carinthia and leave his brother to negotiate the humiliating **Treaty of Passau** in 1552. Charles was entirely

Luther with the reformers. To the right of Luther are Bugenhagen, Erasmus (included for his scholarly achievements), Jonas, Cruziger and Melanchthon; Spalatin and Forster stand to Luther's left. Copy after Lucas Cranach the Younger.

disenchanted by the events that had followed the victory at Mühlberg. Moreover, his financial position had steadily deteriorated; years of warfare and religious strife had taken their toll both physically and materially. By 1555, all religious matters in the empire were in the hands of Ferdinand. Finally, at Augsburg, a pragmatic and workable solution was found whereby Catholicism and Lutheranism were allowed to co-exist within the Empire:

KEY TERM

The Religious Peace of Augsburg, 25 September 1555 was a compromise peace that would last the best part of 250 years. It was governed by the principle of electors, princes and magistrates deciding upon the religion of their subjects. *Ius reformandi*, or the right to reform, lay with the elites.

- Notably, it was the prince of each territory who decided upon the religion of its inhabitants. Therefore, the political autonomy of the princes was effectively recognised. On the back of the Reformation their power and influence had increased.
- The crucial decree within the **Religious Peace of Augsburg** was *cuius regio, eius religio*. In short, he who ruled the principality would decree its religion.
- Emigration was the answer for those committed Catholics who found themselves in a Lutheran state or vice versa. Yet, in reality, the Peace merely recognised what had been the situation on the ground for the previous two decades.
- Importantly, the Peace specifically mentioned Lutheranism and no freedom of worship was to be granted to any other form of religion. More radical groups such as the Anabaptists were not recognised and, more importantly, there was no mention of Calvinism (see Chapter 6). The year 1555 also marked John Calvin's triumph in Geneva and the international impact of that faith was perhaps more marked and widespread than that of Lutheranism.

Indeed, although the Religious Peace of Augsburg remained intact for the next 63 years, the second wave of reform initiated by Calvin and the growing Catholic response meant that religious strife in Europe had only just begun.

CONCLUSION

It is clear, therefore, that the spectacular successes of Lutheranism in the 1520s were consolidated by the princes after 1530:

- Large territorial gains were made, but the movement lost its exuberant popular edge.
- Lutheranism became, for some princes, a vehicle for political power or material wealth. Indeed, one could argue that the movement failed to fulfil its early promise, and outside Germany and Scandinavia, its gains were few.
- Co-operation and union with other Protestant groups, such as the Zwinglians, had proved impossible, thereby perhaps diluting the overall challenge to Catholicism.
- Luther's energy and idealism of the early 1520s gave way to stubbornness and frustration.

The narrative of the German Reformation after 1530 can almost be told without mention of its figurehead. One could argue that Luther had always been a conservative reformer, yet the extent to which the movement had become politicised under the princes can be illustrated by the fact that, at Augsburg in 1555, they were given the decision on which faith to adopt. Luther had laid down his theology in the 1520s and, while still involved in church organisation, much of that work was being carried out by Melanchthon, Bugenhagen and others. Nevertheless, what had been unimaginable in 1500 had occurred by 1555: the people of the Empire could now choose between two Christian faiths.

SUMMARY QUESTIONS

1 How important was princely support in the consolidation of Lutheran gains?

2 Why was Charles V unable to deal effectively with the Lutheran threat?

3 How important was Charles V's military victory at Mühlberg?

4 What was the significance of the Religious Peace of Augsburg of 1555?

CHAPTER 5

The Radical Reformation: Zwingli and the Reformation in Zurich

HULDRYCH ZWINGLI

Outside Germany, the Reformation spread and diversified. Huldrych Zwingli (1484–1531) had already emerged as one of the leading humanists within the Swiss Confederation when he arrived in Zurich in 1519 to become priest of that city.

The beliefs of Zwingli

Zwingli's sermons in those early years as people's priest continued to reflect his humanist past.

Painting of Huldrych Zwingli by Hans Asper, 1549.

- Erasmian criticisms of the superstitious nature of Catholicism were preached.
- Above all else, direct contact with the Bible and the word of God was emphasised.
- However, between 1520 and 1522, Zwingli adopted the doctrines of justification by faith alone and *sola scriptura* (scriptural authority), thereby aligning himself closely with Luther.

Zwingli later stressed that any similarities were a coincidence, and it is debatable just how greatly Zwingli was influenced by the German reformer.

Zwingli the reformer

Zwingli's status and standing as a reformer grew in 1522 when he openly defended a case of fast breaking during Lent, delivering a sermon entitled *On Choice and Liberty in Food*. Moreover, by the end of 1522 he had broken the vows of clerical celibacy. Nothing in these actions or opinions varies greatly from Luther, indeed the similarities are striking. Within Zurich, a split was beginning to become apparent on the city council and among the populace. The split was between:

- those in favour of reform who wanted a quicker pace of change
- the traditional Catholics who had already seen enough reform for their liking.

In January 1523, a disputation was called by the Zurich city council, which intended to restore order by deciding upon the legitimacy of Zwingli's preaching. The local bishop, the Bishop of Constance, refused to attend such a lay gathering. Zwingli, however, prepared for the disputation his **Sixty-Seven Theses**. Although his theses were largely ignored, the Council did call for preaching in the city to be based on the word of God. The principle of evangelical preaching based on the Gospel had been endorsed by a secular power – that is, the Zurich city council.

The Reformation in Zurich

Zwingli now had a more favourable environment in which to operate and introduce further reform. On 15 June 1524, all images were removed from the city, and in December the monasteries of the city were secularised. Finally, in June 1525, the Mass was abolished and replaced by a fully reformed **Lord's Supper**. The Reformation in Zurich had moved swiftly, but across the rest of the Swiss Confederation there was initially less enthusiasm. The five states of central Switzerland re-affirmed their commitment to Catholicism. Yet in Berne, the largest and most powerful state, there was a more favourable reaction. The Mass was abolished there in 1528, while one year later Basle, greatly influenced by the reformer Johannes Oecolampadius, threw in its lot with the Reformation also. By 1529 only one-third of the Swiss population lived in Catholic states.

Zwingli wished to see the spread of the Reformation, and he was willing to endorse military force to do so if necessary. Two camps were clearly emerging within the Swiss Confederation, as it drifted towards civil war. The Catholic states backed by Habsburg aid were potentially formidable. However, both sides were unenthusiastic about the prospect of a bloody civil conflict over religion.

The Sixty-Seven Theses were a statement of Zwingli's doctrine intended for academic debate.

Lord's Supper Holy Communion. Both Luther and Zwingli rejected transubstantiation, yet whilst Luther believed in the real presence of Christ for the true believer, Zwingli saw the Lord's Supper as a purely symbolic service.

- **First Kappel War, 1529.** This was demonstrated by the bloodless First Kappel War in which neither army was willing to encroach upon enemy territory.
- **Second Kappel War, 1531.** The Second Kappel War of 1531 was more conclusive. Divisions within the Reformed side existed between Zurich, which wished to use direct military action and Berne, which favoured an economic blockade of the five central states. These divisions were made worse by the inability of Luther and Zwingli to agree on the degree of real presence in the Eucharist. Therefore the Reformers were deprived of Schmalkaldic assistance in their fight against the Catholic states. In October 1531, Zwingli's forces were routed at the Battle of Kappel and Zwingli was among those killed.

The peace treaties that followed described Catholicism as the true, undoubted faith and conversion to Protestantism was forbidden. However, no attempt was made to return Zurich and Berne to the Catholic fold and Zwinglianism lived on in the north of Switzerland and smaller pockets in the south, before the arrival of Calvinism in the 1540s lessened its significance.

A COMPARISON OF ZWINGLI AND LUTHER

There are a number of similarities and differences between the two reformers:

- **Academic ability.** Unquestionably, these two reformers appear to differ little. Both demonstrated outstanding academic ability and both entered a life in the clergy.
- **Influences.** Zwingli was greatly influenced by humanist professors such as Thomas Wittenbach at the University of Basle and, like Luther, he devoted himself to learning Greek and translating scripture. Moreover, both were influenced by Erasmus, with Zwingli first reading his works in 1516, by which time Luther was well acquainted with the works of the famous humanist and was on the verge, albeit unknowingly, of sparking off the German Reformation.
- **Impact.** Here lies the first major and very obvious

difference. Despite being only a year older, Luther made his impact earlier and more explosively than Zwingli. The message of the two reformers in terms of church reform was very similar and, in some respects, Zwingli was overshadowed by the early impact Luther had made. For example, by 1521 Luther had been condemned by both Emperor and Pope and Lutheranism was evolving as a powerful force within the towns. In 1521, Zwingli had only just begun to become noticed as a public reforming figure in Zurich, and was just coming to terms with justification by faith alone and *sola scriptura*.

- **Environment.** The very environment in which Luther was reforming was, as we have seen, most helpful in developing and spreading his message. Zwingli, on the other hand, could not call on the culturally advanced and semi-literate cities to help his ideas to evolve. The Swiss message was therefore always going to be slow to develop and spread. Another problem for Zwingli was that following so closely in the footsteps of Luther was also likely to dilute the appeal of Zwinglianism. However, Zwingli's influence did slowly spread into south Germany, to cities such as Strasburg and Memmingen. Yet any chance of expansion here was limited because, in turning to the ideas of the Swiss, Zwingli may have isolated these cities politically and economically from the Holy Roman Empire. Therefore, while both men acted as figureheads for reform, it was inevitable that Luther would front the larger and more successful movement.

- **Similarities of doctrine.** The similarities between the two men should perhaps have allowed for a unification of the two strands of Protestantism. Doctrinally they agreed on the path to salvation, while both stressed the duty of the subject to obey his lord. Luther's political influence in Wittenberg may have been greater, but the endorsement of the city council in Zurich was crucial to Zwingli's success.

- **Doctrinal differences.** One issue in particular divided Luther and Zwingli, preventing a united Protestant front. Over the sacrament of the Eucharist and in particular the words of Christ, *Hoc est corpus meum*, no agreement could be found. Luther's position, as we have already seen, was relatively conservative, in that he

KEY TERM

Hoc est corpus meum is the Latin for 'This is my body'. This term is at the heart of the Mass for, at this moment, the priest offers the bread as a symbol of Christ's body.

KEY THEME

Personal rivalry of Zwingli and Luther One should not forget that there was a strong element of personal rivalry in the doctrinal debate between Luther and Zwingli. Each believed himself to be a prophet. Indeed, Luther saw Zwingli as a rival and he detested all competition.

denied the element of sacrifice in the Catholic sacrament and the notion of a miracle taking place, but he did stress that the body of Christ was physically present in the Eucharist. For Zwingli, the sacrament was purely symbolic, and the real presence was denied. By 1529, it became clear that a solution was required and, to this end, Philip of Hesse invited both **Zwingli and Luther** to Marburg in order to debate the issue. Already, Luther had outlined his position personally in print to Zwingli in an aggressive work entitled *Confession on Christ's Supper* (1528). Agreement was impossible and the chance for unity lost. The south German cities returned to the Lutheran fold through the Four Cities Confession of 1530 and then later with the Wittenberg Concord of 1536.

CONCLUSION

Ultimately, one should not view Zwingli as a radical. Luther regarded him as such because of his denial of the real presence and his endorsement of military force to further the Word of God, the latter being a position which Luther himself would have adopted by 1537. Zwingli did manage to oversee a disciplined and bloodless reformation in Zurich, which was consolidated by Heinrich Bullinger. Moreover, the close co-operation between Church and State, which Zwingli had encouraged, was later to be replicated by Calvin in Geneva.

SUMMARY QUESTIONS

1 What was the impact of Zwinglian reform in Switzerland?

2 In what respects was Zwinglianism more radical than Lutheranism?

3 How did Luther and Zwingli differ over the Eucharist?

4 How significant was the Colloquy of Marburg in the future development of Protantism in Europe?

CHAPTER 6

What is the significance of the Anabaptists and John Calvin?

What are the ideas of the Anabaptists?

Essentially, the Anabaptists were the real radicals of the early Reformation in Europe. They represented a small and extremely diverse group of the population that had become discontented with the moderate nature of mainstream reform. Luther and Zwingli had initiated Church reform, but some believed that they had failed to see it through to its natural end:

- For the Anabaptists, Luther had been too conservative and had bowed to authority on too many occasions, leaving a church that was little better than before.
- Allegiance to Rome had been shattered but, according to the Anabaptists, further reform was required through which certainty of faith and commitment to a Christian lifestyle could be assured.
- Zwingli called this group Anabaptist (from 'anti-Baptists') as a consequence of their rejection of infant baptism. **Anabaptists** were re-baptisers, in that they believed in adult baptism, because only with maturity and experience could one understand the significance of this sacrament.
- The Anabaptist movement was a wide-ranging one and tended to attract fanatical **demagogues** who played upon the Anabaptists' belief that visions and inner voices constituted a direct line with God.

Instances of violence and immorality in south Germany in 1525, north Germany in 1534, as well as in the Swiss cantons and the Netherlands, tarnished Anabaptism with an extremist and dangerous brush. This view was unfair as the violence and immorality were practised by a small minority. Anabaptism began as a spiritual, intellectual and pacifistic movement, which was hijacked by extremist figureheads. Despite ferocious persecution, Anabaptism continued to flourish in the Netherlands and, later, in America.

Thomas Müntzer (1489–1525). Trained as a priest, Müntzer was a conventional supporter of Luther in Saxony, before becoming more radical in his defence of the Zwickau Prophets in 1521. In July 1524, he preached a sermon in which he revealed his belief in direct communication with God through dreams and visions. Apparently he was one of the 'godly' and now it was time to turn on the ungodly with force. Müntzer's followers were generally from the lower classes of society; attracted by his message of equality and redistribution of wealth. In 1524, he moved to Mühlhausen, which was at the centre of the Peasants' Revolt. In alliance with Heinrich Pfeiffer, they had overthrown the city council and were beginning to restore lands to the peasantry through force. Yet in May 1525, the revolt was abruptly stopped when the peasant armies were routed outside Frankenhausen. Müntzer was captured, tortured and killed.

The North German and Dutch Anabaptists. The most important Anabaptist leader was Melchior Hoffmann (d. 1543), who was based in Emden in East Friesland. Hoffmann and his followers re-baptised hundreds of people in the Netherlands. His ideas spread to north German towns such as Münster and Cologne. Hoffmann preached an **apocalyptic message**:

- He claimed that he was the **prophet Elijah** and that the world would end in 1533.
- He also argued that the ungodly needed to be cleansed before the Second Coming of Christ.
- However, he did not suggest the use of force in purifying the community, stating rather conservatively that only **magistrates** should use the sword.
- Strasburg was to be the gathering point for the godly where the end of the world would be awaited.

Yet the Last Days did not come, and when a self-professed prophet outlives judgement day, his followers tend to lose faith. Hoffman died in prison in 1543. However, his apprentices were to prove more radical.

Münster. Many of Hoffmann's supporters did maintain a belief in Anabaptism, which was continued in the Westphalian town of Münster in 1533. Hundreds were

---

KEY TERM

Apocalyptic message This is a message that predicts that the end of the world is coming soon.

KEY PERSON

The prophet Elijah is an important figure in the Old Testament part of the Bible. Elijah argued for the worship of God rather than pagan gods.

KEY TERM

Magistrates are those who made up the ruling oligarchy of sixteenth-century towns.

attracted to northwest Germany from the Netherlands, including Jan van Leiden, a Dutch tailor. Under the guidance of the reformer Bernard Rothmann, Münster began to move towards Anabaptism. Over 1400 people in Münster were re-baptised. In February 1533, the Anabaptists took power in the town of Münster with their leader Jan Mathijs being voted into power. However, the prince bishop of Münster laid siege to the city in February 1534, a siege that lasted 16 months. In many ways this military threat further radicalised the stance of those within the city walls. All those who did not want to join the Anabaptists were encouraged to leave the city, while all private property was abolished and historical records destroyed. So convinced was the Anabaptist leader, Jan Matthijs, that the second coming was near and that the kingdom of God was to be founded in Münster that he charged headlong into the besieging troops, and was killed.

Jan van Leiden. His successor was Jan van Leiden who introduced an Old Testament kingship based on **polygamy** and dictatorial rule. King Jan was the self-proclaimed new King David in the New Jerusalem of Münster. He took 16 wives and the immorality and harsh rule that followed did much to harm the reputation of Anabaptism. With food running low and morale dropping daily, the city was eventually betrayed from within on 25 June 1535. The troops entered the city and brutally tortured and killed the inhabitants. Jan van Leiden was paraded around northern Germany before being killed in January 1536 in the market place of Münster, while others were beheaded before being exhibited in iron cages that hung from the city church as an example to others of what became of such radicals. Anabaptism never really recovered from such a blow, and the movement split into several factions. The most successful of these factions were the pacifist followers of **Menno Simons** in the Netherlands.

CALVIN'S BACKGROUND

John Calvin was born in Noyon in Picardy, a region in northeastern France, on 10 July 1509. Twenty-six years younger than Luther, he was more radical in his doctrine

KEY TERM

Polygamy is the practice of having more than one husband or wife at a time.

KEY PERSON

Menno Simons endured the survival of a more moderate brand of Anabaptism during a period (1536–61) of severe persecution. Through his missionary work in Germany and Netherlands, he spread the doctrine of adult baptism and the rejection of clerical oaths. By 1572, the Mennonites had been granted toleration in the Netherlands and part of Germany.

and the founder of a more widely influential branch of Protestantism. Luther and Zwingli had paved the way for reform. Indeed, it is worth noting that Calvin was only 20 when, in 1529, the second Diet of Speyer witnessed the protestation of the princes and the Marburg Colloquy demonstrated the division between German and Swiss churches. He developed his theology in an environment that had already witnessed Luther's challenge to the traditional institutions of the Catholic Church and in some ways this made his task easier. However, between 1538 and 1564 he:

- gave Protestantism an institutional structure
- worked tirelessly to mould a reformed city in Geneva and to spread the message further afield.

John Calvin, contemporary painting c.1540.

Calvin matriculated at the University of Paris in 1523, graduating with an MA in 1528. However, on his father's orders, he began to study the law, attending lectures at Orleans and Bourges, before returning to Paris in 1531. As a linguistic expert in Latin, Hebrew and Greek, he attended the renowned humanist academy in Paris known as the *Collège de France*. The young, gifted and serious-minded Calvin published his *Commentary on Seneca* in 1532. In it he emphasised the role of scripture, especially the epistles of St Paul and St Augustine. It was around this time that Calvin underwent a conversion experience. From now on he genuinely believed that:

- God had turned his life in a new direction and was teaching to his heart;
- he was one of the elect, chosen by God to carry out his orders and that everything he did was for the grace of God and in His name.

His conversion was sudden and clear cut.

Shortly after this, however, in January 1535, Calvin was forced to flee France after a number of perilous developments initiated by a fiery sermon delivered by his friend **Nicholas Cop**, the newly-elected rector of Paris University, in November 1533. Cop's sermon stressed the need for church reform based on the authority of scripture and it was received as potentially dangerous by Francis I. Up until this point, Francis had patronised humanist thought within France and his sister, Margaret of Navarre, was even a part of the humanist intellectual circle that had developed at Meaux during the 1520s.

After October 1534, such toleration disappeared due to the excesses of Antoine Marcourt, who plastered copies of his rude, crude and insulting theses against the Catholic Mass all over Paris. It is even claimed that Marcourt managed to place copies in the King's bedchamber at Amboise. Marcourt's views were those of a minority, but they frightened the king into a period of harsh repression. The so-called 'Day of the Placards' saw Calvin leave for safety in Basle. It was while he was there that he wrote the important work, *Institution de la Religion Chrétienne* (Institutes of the Christian Religion). Never before had a

KEY PERSON

Nicholas Cop As rector of the University of Paris, he delivered a controversial sermon on All Saints' Day, 1533, which alluded to the ideas of Lefèvre d'Etaples, the French humanist and evangelical. Fearing repercussions, Cop fled into exile and Calvin followed.

Protestant reformer produced such a clear or structured presentation of doctrine and the true Christian life. The Institutes were written as a commentary on scripture, which he regarded as the highest human knowledge. What began as a six-chapter introduction to Christian faith in 1536, ended up as an 80-chapter masterpiece by 1559, and had immense international influence.

Calvin's theology

These are the main points of theology outlined by Calvin in the Institutes.

- **God.** Stress was laid upon the omnipotence and omnipresence of God. He was all-knowing and all-powerful and He intervened in daily life. The highest human knowledge is that of God, and obedience to God's will is the primal human duty. Through **Adam's fall** man had lost power and goodness and as a consequence no human work can be seen as having merit in God's eyes. It therefore follows that Calvin believed in justification by faith alone, whereby good works contributed nothing to salvation, whereas God's gift of faith was all-important.
- **Predestination.** Following on from this doctrine was the stress that Calvin laid upon predestination, and this became the central core of Calvinist theology. Calvin argued that all good is of God and man was either saved or lost through divine choice. In short, God had predestined (pre-decided) that some men were to be saved and others to be condemned. It was God's choice as to who the elect (saved) were and who were the reprobates (damned). Indeed, Calvin believed in double predestination – that is, God had chosen the elect *and* the reprobates.

To many, Calvin's theology appeared harsh and indeed some problems with predestination were raised such as if God was all good, he cannot have willed the fall of man starting with Adam's fall, yet if he was all powerful it could not have happened without his knowledge. For Calvin, the doctrine of predestination was meant to be a comforting one, reassuring people that God had a plan of salvation for them. However, for many it raised uncertainties as to whether they were one of the elect or not. Calvin maintained that man must always work hard to come nearer to God through study of scripture and by leading a morally pure life. Nevertheless, one could not tell whether one belonged to the elect or the reprobates. Under persecution, such a doctrine was comforting, in that the Calvinist community was inspired to carry on the struggle in the knowledge that they were the godly and they were the elect, chosen by God to be saved, as opposed to the Catholics who were to be damned. Such reassurance was evidently appreciated both in France and the Netherlands during the second half of the sixteenth century. Yet in a settled Calvinist society, such a doctrine was less assuring.

- **The structure of the Calvinist Church.** The Church on earth was not hierarchical and, according to Calvin, the New Testament recognises as church officers only pastors, doctors, deacons and lay elders, who serve with the assent of the congregation.
- **Disciplinary role.** The Church was to have a disciplinary role with independent jurisdiction from civil courts. This included the right to excommunicate. Therefore, Church courts were to make the decision over the right of an individual to attend communion. For punishments that went beyond excommunication, the civil authorities were to intervene.
- **The sacraments.** Calvin recognised only two sacraments as having any scriptural backing, namely baptism and the Eucharist. Like Luther and Zwingli, he rejected the Catholic doctrine of transubstantiation and, in terms of Christ's presence in the Eucharist, he stood between Zurich and Wittenberg. Like Zwingli, he denied any real presence at communion, asserting that Christ was in heaven. However, he did also state that, to the believer, Christ was spiritually present. In short, Calvin argued that a real but spiritual presence was received by faith.

In conclusion, it is clear that the key to understanding the Institutes was the integration of Church, State and sacraments in maintaining a true Christian life.

The impact of Calvin's ideas

Much of what Calvin put forward was not original and could be found in the epistles of St Paul and St Augustine. Many of his ideas had been argued by Luther. Yet the emphasis he placed on predestination was shocking and novel. Moreover, as he revealed in 1541 in the *Ecclesiastical Ordinances*, it was the institutional organisation and structure of the proposed Calvinist church that was most revolutionary. The most controversial element was the independent disciplinary role of the church. Throughout the 1540s and 1550s, Calvin set about reforming Geneva as a model Christian city. Many came to criticise the perceived puritanical and harsh disciplinary code enforced there; yet, by 1560, few could deny the extent of Calvin's achievements:

- He remodelled this city state along the lines of the *Institutes and Ordinances*, and triumphed over opposing political factions.
- He set Geneva up as a refuge for exiled Calvinists from France.

Influence abroad. The influence of Calvin and Geneva over the development of French Protestantism was profound. Moreover, although he was personally less involved in the Netherlands, Calvinism emerged as the official state religion in the northern United Provinces by 1609. Similarly, in Scotland and in 28 states of the Empire, most significantly the Palatinate, Calvinism was adopted by the ruling elites. Furthermore, American **Puritanism** and Scottish **Presbyterianism** were both offshoots of Calvinism. Nevertheless, despite such international success, one must remember that in the Netherlands and France Calvinism developed on the back of serious civil unrest and, in both countries, it was only ever a 10 per cent minority that supported the cause.

KEY TERMS

Puritanism is a movement concerned with the purification of ceremony within the Church and the following of a strict moral code.

Presbyterianism is the form of Church government by presbyters or elders, in which a strict moral order is enforced.

SUMMARY QUESTIONS

1 What was Anabaptism?

2 Why did Jan Mathijs fail to establish a New Jerusalem in Münster?

3 List and explain the main ideas of Calvin.

CHAPTER 7

The Catholic Reformation

INTRODUCTION: COUNTER REFORMATION OR CATHOLIC REFORMATION?

The actions taken by the Catholic Church in reaction to the success of Lutheranism have often been labelled as the Counter Reformation. In particular, Protestant historians have often used this term to describe the measures adopted by Catholic princes and new religious orders in the second half of the sixteenth century, which won back not only Catholic lands but also hearts and minds. At the heart of this Catholic counter-attack was the Council of Trent, a General Council of the Church, which met in northern Italy in three sessions between 1545 and 1563. Yet to many Catholic historians, the term Counter Reformation is an inadequate one as it implies that change only came about in response to the Protestant Reformation, and it takes no account of the widespread spiritual reform movements within Catholicism before Luther. In many ways the historian **A.G. Dickens** simplifies the issue by maintaining that it was obviously both a Counter Reformation and a Catholic Reformation. Some elements of positive renewal are evident before Luther, while a Counter Reformation in response to the impact of Lutheranism is also discernible. Another historian, **Hubert Jedin**, agrees with Dickens, adding that the defence of Catholicism in the Counter Reformation built upon older ideas formulated before Luther and therefore one should interconnect the two terms rather than treat them separately.

> ### KEY HISTORIANS
>
> **A.G. Dickens** explains his ideas in *The Counter Reformation* (Thames and Hudson, 1968). **Hubert Jedin's** views were expressed a generation earlier in *Catholic Reformation or Counter Reformation?* (1946).

WHAT WAS THE NATURE OF CATHOLIC REFORM BEFORE THE COUNCIL OF TRENT (1545–63)?

Between 1400 and 1545, Catholic reform was based on a local level rather than a papal one. Moreover, advocates of reform were generally backward and conservative rather than innovative. Spiritual renewal and revitalisation were based upon a restoration of supposed past high standards, and it is in this light that we ought to consider the emergence of Catholic lay brotherhoods, or confraternities, and new religious orders during the late fifteenth century. The aims of brotherhoods were to pray, fast and serve God, neighbour and the Church. In doing so, such reformers would set an example to the disadvantaged around them. Many of these brotherhoods were to be found in Italy, although their establishment had nothing to do with the papacy.

The Oratory of Divine Love. The most famous brotherhood was the **Oratory of Divine Love**, established in Genoa in 1497 by the layman **Ettore Vernazza** for the inward renewal of its members through religious exercises (prayer and meditation) and distribution of charity. Similar groups sprang up in Rome, Bologna and Naples, taking the same name. The Oratory in Rome nurtured future leaders of the Catholic reform movement such as Thiene, Giberti and Sadoleto. In particular, two prominent members of the Oratory should be noted.

- One was **Gian Pietro Carafa** who, along with **Cajetan da Thiene**, founded the Theatine Order and devoted most of his adult life to the eradication of Lutheranism. At the head of the zelanti movement, which pursued a hard line on Protestantism, he was influential in the reorganisation of the Spanish Inquisition and the drawing up of an Index of Prohibited Books. In 1555, Carafa became Pope Paul IV.
- Another member of the Oratory was **Gasparo Contarini**, a Venetian diplomat and ambassador to Charles V. Contarini was a lay, liberal Catholic reformer who stressed the importance of reform from within the Catholic Church and of justification by faith alone. Contarini was made a Cardinal in 1535 and Paul III saw him as an important figurehead for church reform. Later he would incur suspicion due to his belief in the Augustinian version of the Pauline doctrine on salvation, but not before he had attempted to negotiate a compromise with the Lutherans at Regensburg in 1541. Contarini and other reformers like him in Italy were

known as *spirituali,* due to their wish for serious reform of the Church and the way in which they embraced the Gospel and, in particular, the ideas of St Augustine, devoting their lives to following Christ.

The Oratory is therefore important, because out of this holy club emerged devout laymen who would play an important role in future Catholic regeneration and defend Catholicism against future Lutheran attack. Moreover, new orders such as the Theatine Order developed from the Oratory, providing a more zealous and active alternative to old-style monasticism. Finally, within the Oratory, we can witness different reactions to Lutheranism in the 1530s and 1540s between the spirituali, who were more liberal and favoured a compromise settlement to restore unity, and the *zelanti,* who endorsed a more hard-line attitude of destruction.

WHAT WERE THE NEW ORDERS AND WHAT WAS THEIR IMPACT ON REFORM?

Thus, from lay confraternities came new orders, often functioning on lower social levels at the beginning of the sixteenth century. Monks, nuns and friars were under fire for their inwardly comfortable existence and their lack of pastoral care for the local community. In short, monasticism was being portrayed as out of date and redundant in matters of Church reform. New orders placed an emphasis on spiritual not institutional renewal, based on the principles of simplicity and humility. Social and pastoral care were seen as important, motivated by the Gospel and the example of Christ. An example of such an order would be the Somaschi, founded in 1530 by the Venetian nobleman Girolamo Miani and devoted to charity and the care of the sick and needy. Hospitals were established in Venice, Verona and Milan, demonstrating their practical commitment to following Christ. Another order was the Barnabites. Founded by three north-Italian laymen and inspired by the teachings of St Paul, they became renowned for large-scale open-air meetings in which the word of God would be preached to the masses. The Theatines (see above), founded in 1524, was another

KEY PEOPLE

Cajetan da Thiene (1480–1547) Ordained in 1516, he entered the Oratory of St Jerome in Venice. Disaffected by the moral laxity of the clergy, he founded the Theatine Order, which allowed the regular clergy to live in the community, yet still be bound by vows. Committed to pastoral care and a restoration of proper religious feeling among the community, Cajetan was canonized in 1671 for his efforts towards reform.

Gasparo Contarini (1483–1542) Having studied at Padua, Contarini returned to his birthplace, Venice, and immediately took up government office in that republic. In 1520, he became an ambassador to the court of Charles V. In 1535, Pope Paul III made him a cardinal and, from there, Contarini led a commission recommending papal reform. He also travelled to Germany as papal legate.

Gasparo Contarini, the great liberal Catholic reformer.

society of priests who received training as reformers and who placed an emphasis on pastoral work and active good works. The Theatines still took monastic vows and maintained a rule of poverty, but lived and worked in the community.

It should be noted that these orders are significant because they show that a reform movement did exist within the Catholic Church before the advance of Protestantism. Yet their aims were very traditional, based around past devotional principles and visions, such as service to God and one's neighbour. Orders such as the Theatines still observed old Franciscan principles of poverty, while the Somaschi returned to the spirit of St Francis in their care for the dying. The orders were honourable, active and pious, but hardly striking or even forward in outlook. Although not founded for the purpose of counteracting Lutheranism, it would be Protestant advances that changed the outlook of such orders and broadened their horizons. In particular, this can be applied to the two most important new orders, namely the Capuchins and the Jesuits.

The Capuchins

Established in Camerino in 1528, the Capuchins were reformed Franciscans combining poverty and austerity with a skill for preaching. The movement was established around Matteo da Bascio, a young Italian Observant Franciscan who wished to follow the example of **St Francis** and preach the Gospel in a simple manner to the people. Bascio even wore a pointed hood or *cappuccio* to imitate his saintly example. From humble beginnings, the Capuchins grew to nearly 30,000 members and 1500 houses in the seventeenth century. The Capuchins were stricter and more zealous than the other branch of the Franciscans, namely the Observants, who tried to sideline and destroy the Capuchins. Their failure to do so was due to powerful support from individuals such as the Duchess of Camerin, the niece of Pope Clement VII. Even the betrayal of their vicar-general, **Bernardino Ochino**, who became a Protestant in 1541, failed to halt their progress and influence. The Capuchin service towards the sick was legendary in northern Italy where they fearlessly served plague victims with no thought for their own well-being.

KEY PEOPLE

St Francis of Assisi (1181–1226) Francesco Bernardone, the son of a wealthy draper from Assisi who was disowned by his father in 1207 after selling some of his goods to pay for the repair of the local church at San Damiano. In 1210 Pope Innocent III gave him authority to become an itinerant preacher along with 11 companions. Based near Assisi the Friars Manor, Lesser Brothers began and developed into a significant religious order throughout Italy promoting humbleness, equality and the word of God. St Francis was canonized in 1228.

Bernardino Ochino (1487–1564) Originally an Observant Franciscan from Siena, he joined the newly established Capuchins in 1534. In 1538 he was elected as general of the order, gaining recognition as a wonderful preacher. Yet his ideas became more and more radical, and he displayed his religious heterodoxy in Naples where he joined Peter Martyr Vermigli. Under suspicion from the authorities, Ochino fled to Calvinist Geneva where he embraced Protestantism. Later in his life it would be Zwinglianism rather than Calvinism that would hold greater appeal for Ochino.

The Catholic Reformation   77

Yet, again, one might argue that the Capuchins remained within an earlier tradition and it was the Jesuit commitment to ministry which singled them out as the most outward-going and important of the new orders.

The Jesuits

The Jesuits were founded in 1540 by a Spaniard named Ignatius Loyola, who was born in the Basque country in 1490 to a middling noble family. Wounded in both legs by a cannonball while defending Pamplona from the French, Loyola underwent a conversion experience as he recovered in hospital. He reflected on the life of Christ and

Portrait of Ignatius Loyola c.1622, attributed to Juan de Roelas.

the saints, recognising how inadequate man was before a pure and majestic God. Once recovered, he headed for Barcelona to take ship for Jerusalem. On the way to Barcelona, he stopped at the Benedictine monastery of Montserrat, where he made a confession of his life and prayed to Our Lady, guarding her statue assiduously. He then spent eleven months living as a hermit in a cavern near Manresa. There, Loyola sought consolation through prayer and fasting.

Yet ultimately, Loyola held great doubts about the route to salvation and his own inadequacies. On the brink of suicide he found reconciliation through visions of God. In particular, the Holy Trinity was illuminated and God's creation of the world was revealed to him. Rejuvenated, Loyola made it to the Holy Land, where he intended to begin his crusade to convert the Moslem world, although the political situation there meant he could stay for only 20 days. He returned to educate himself in Spain and train for the priesthood in the universities of Alcala and Salamanca. He lived off alms and his preaching and religious conversions even brought him before the Inquisition.

To avoid further danger, he moved to the University of Paris in 1528, where he studied until 1535. It was here that Loyola expanded his horizons and gathered around him a core of permanent companions. Among them were fellow Spaniards such as Francis Xavier, Diego Laynez, Alfonso Salmeron and Nicholas Alfonso, along with Frenchmen such as Jean Codure. On 15 August 1534, Loyola and six companions climbed to the top of Montmartre and, in the Chapel of St Denis, they made vows of chastity and poverty, promising also to undertake a crusade to the Holy Land. Should the latter be impossible, they agreed to offer their absolute obedience to the Pope in Rome and serve his needs selflessly.

In 1539, Loyola and his companions decided that the only way in which their community could be preserved was through the founding of an order. As a result, Pope Paul III oversaw the founding of the Society of Jesus in 1540, which vowed to work for the advancement of souls through preaching and the ministry of God's Word.

Loyola also brought to the order a scheme of devotion outlined in his work entitled *Spiritual Exercises* (c.1541). The *Exercises* had been outlined in Loyola's mind since his days in Manresa and they were amended and revised until they gained approval by the Church in 1548. The *Exercises* are a manual of instructions for those who make a spiritual retreat intending to have a transforming experience upon life. The work guides the retreatant through a programme of prayer lasting 30 days. The individual is shown his life within the greater context of humanity. The purpose behind the *Exercises* was a practical one, introducing the retreatant to a life of prayer and helping the individual decide upon his vocation and calling in life. Loyola had certainly drawn upon late-medieval literature on meditation and mental prayer in writing the *Exercises*, and he was probably influenced by **Thomas à Kempis'** work, *The Imitation of Christ* (1418) as well as *Exercises of the Spiritual Life* (1500) by Garcia de Cisneros.

The *Exercises* gave militant Jesuits a powerful weapon. Missionaries could argue that ordinary Christians could come close to salvation through individual meditation and exercise of their natural capacities. Ignatius and his company were offering guidance in accordance with divine will, and pastoral missions throughout Europe allowed many to hear the Christian soldier's message. Indeed, the message of the Jesuits would spread to the new world of South America and the Far East. They were also important in maintaining Catholic unity in the south of Europe and conquering some lands in the north.

The Jesuits were regarded as one of the most dynamic and effective orders of the Counter Reformation, yet one should not forget that their origins lay in the spirituality of the early Catholic Reformation. By the time Loyola died in 1556, the Jesuits numbered 1000 members, a figure which peaked in the mid-eighteenth century at 23,000. Moreover, the contribution the Jesuits made to education should not be underestimated, as thousands of young men were prepared for active Christian life in Jesuit colleges.

The Ursulines
Of all the women's congregations, the Ursulines was the

most numerous and influential. It was the first women's congregation committed to the ministry of education. In France especially, they became one of the most important vehicles for Catholic reform, numbering 10,000 in 1750, compared to 3500 Jesuits. The Ursuline order was formed in 1535 in Brescia by Angela Merici. Her vision was to form an order of virgins and widows who would work actively to restore the Church to standards of excellence that existed in the past. Education in particular was seen as crucial, hence the adoption of St Ursula as patron. While young girls were instructed in Christian doctrine, the Ursulines also attended to the sick and needy. Officially recognised in 1544 by Pope Paul III, four years after Angela's death, the Ursulines were revitalised under Charles Borromeo who, as archbishop, brought them to Milan in 1567. In 1576, he demanded that each bishop establish a branch of the Ursulines in his diocese; thus numbers increased throughout northern Italy. By the beginning of the seventeenth century the Ursulines had expanded into France through the papal territory of Avignon. Still the Ursulines lived with families in the community and took no vows. Yet in 1612, the Paris community accepted monastic enclosure and, although the Ursulines were forced to move back into cloister, they received special papal dispensation to carry on their active educational work in the community. The Ursulines were very significant because people realised that young girls would be future mothers and would have an influence on the way in which their children would be brought up.

Conclusion

The new religious orders were important agents of christianisation in the world, through care for the sick, preaching, and especially education. The involvement of laymen and women added a new presence and dimension to the Catholic Church and new opportunities for the congregation. Moreover, the Jesuits in particular put a renewed emphasis on private meditation and vocation as well as guidance on how to arrive at it through the *Exercises*. There is little doubt that the new orders supported papal authority and indeed strengthened it when the Curia came under attack from Luther.

HOW IMPORTANT WERE THE PRINCES IN SPREADING REFORM?

The power to spread and consolidate reform lay with the princes of Europe. Such men were often on the lookout to extend their own power and privileges, and this often came at the expense of the Church. However, as princes gradually became more involved in clerical affairs, so the opportunities to endorse and promote reform arose.

Ximenes. One example of the integration of Church and State for the benefit of the former can be seen in Cardinal Ximenes (1436–1517), a Franciscan who became Archbishop of Toledo in 1495, the most important position in the Spanish Church.

Ferdinand and Isabella of Spain entrusted the reform of friars and nuns to Ximenes and, from his own resources, he founded the University of Alcala to enhance the education of clerics. He welcomed foreign scholars to Spain and encouraged biblical humanism and the retranslation of scripture. Most notable was his endorsement of an Old Testament translation in Greek, Latin and Hebrew, licensed by Leo X in 1520. Ximenes' work as a reformer has become rather overshadowed by the actions of the Spanish Inquisition during this period, in which thousands of Moorish and Jewish converts to Christianity were burned against a background of crusading Spain and intolerance of heresy.

France. In France, the States-General in 1484 and the General Assembly of the French clergy in 1494 denounced abuses and malpractice in the Church. Indeed, while Louis XII and Francis I may have found the conquest of Italy more enticing than Church reform, France did witness influential groups of Christian humanists during these years. A piety closely related to the *devotio moderna* emerged among small groups of upper-class intellectuals.

In Paris, the group centred around Jean Standonck, a Netherlander who re-organised the Collège de Montaigu in 1502, and developed it into a respected headquarters for clerical training. Standonck made the link between classical

KEY TERM

Devotio moderna This literally translates as modern devotion and refers to the revival of spiritual life from the end of the fourteenth century, which spread from ideas originating in the Netherlands to Germany, France and Italy. Such ideas placed stress on the inner life of an individual and encouraged meditation on the life and passion of Christ.

learning and a disciplined life, arguing that a combination of the two was necessary for any priest. Another significant individual in the French Church was Cardinal Georges d'Amboise (d. 1510), who reformed and disciplined the French religious orders in 1501. As parties of armed men expelled monks from monasteries in St Germain, d'Amboise became aware of the financial gains that could be made from dissolving religious houses; profits which could be used to finance the costly Italian Wars.

Humanism

One should not forget the humanists when discussing early church reform. Humanism was the application of classical studies to life and letters, encouraging devotion to the common good and participation in government. Greek or the classical Latin of Cicero was the language used by these scholars, who took up a renewed interest in the early Christian sources and scriptures. While the Renaissance of the fourteenth century witnessed a revival of classical literature and the expansion of knowledge, the sixteenth century saw humanism become associated with Church reform, a call led by the foremost of all humanists, Desiderius Erasmus.

Erasmus wrote sceptically and cynically of the state of monasticism in his *Praise of Folly* (1509), yet such criticisms had existed for decades before Erasmus. More important was his mastery of Latin and Greek, which paved the way for a Greek New Testament in 1516. For some historians, Erasmus and others like him laid the foundations of anti-clericalism upon which Luther built. Yet Erasmus was no friend of heresy and was merely advocating reform from within the Catholic Church. While he may have had initial sympathy with Luther over the indulgences controversy (see page 24), he demonstrated his ultimate loyalty to the Catholic Church in 1525, when he wrote against Luther in *On the Freedom of the Will.*

It is also worth noting that nearly all the early Catholic champions who replied to Luther's challenge through works and preaching were educated and reared in a humanist tradition. Johannes Eck, Thomas More, John Fisher, Johannes Cochlaeus, Josse van Clichtove and

Erasmus himself were formidable opponents of Luther who used their literary and intellectual skills to fuel the early Catholic counter-attack. Other younger humanists, such as Melanchthon, sided with the Protestants.

Conclusion

After 1525, the humanists became less significant Catholic champions, as confessional lines hardened. Moreover, Charles V increasingly recognised that his search for religious unity in the Holy Roman Empire was futile. By the time that Charles V turned his attentions towards reform it was too late. Many princes and cities had already embraced the ideas of Luther, and Charles eventually endorsed a compromise with the Protestants at Regensburg in 1541. Predictably, the attempt to find a theological middle ground had failed and now he had to look to the papacy to call a General Council of the Church in order to spread reform. Luther had called upon the princes to usher in reform in 1520, and many such as Philip of Hesse had answered his call positively. Charles V could not trust the princes of the Empire and so it was to the papacy that his attention now turned.

HOW EXTENSIVE WAS PAPAL REFORM BETWEEN 1400 AND 1545?

Renaissance popes have a poor reputation as power hungry, worldly figureheads with little interest in reform. Up to a point this is true, as illustrated by the pontificate of Alexander VI, who led a decadent life and even oversaw the burning of the Florentine reformer Savonarola (see page 9). Moreover, neither Leo X nor Clement VII was quick or decisive in his reaction to Luther and, for both popes, it was the fortunes of their house (Medici) and of their city (Florence) that were of primary importance. Yet popes also had great political concerns during the early modern period as, since the Great Schism of the fourteenth century, the power of the papacy had been questioned by princes and bishops. Many believed that General Councils should be called to govern the Church and that the power of the popes should be reduced. The **Councils of Constance** (1414–7) and **Basle** (1431–49) saw the views of

KEY EVENTS

The Council of Constance (1414–7) Convoked by Pope John XXIII at the behest of Emperor Sigismund, the purpose of the Council was to end the Great Schism which had resulted in three popes in 1414 (Gregory XII, Benedict XIII and John XXIII)! This was achieved with the election of a compromise candidate in Martin V but, in the context of reform, the Council set an interesting precedent in calling for a General Council after the next five, seven and ten years. Such a council would discuss and propose reform and was clearly a threat to papal supremacy.

The Council of Basle (1431–49) Presided over by Eugenius IV, this Council carried over anti-papal sentiments from Constance and reaffirmed the decrees of that Council on the superiority of a General Council over the Pope. An anxious Eugenius transferred the Council to Ferrarra in order to tighten his control. Those who remained in Basle deposed Eugenius and, in his place, elected Amadeus of Saxony as Felix V. The major powers, however, recognised Eugenius and were keen to avoid another schism.

The Popes 1484–1655

Innocent VIII	August 1484 – July 1492
Alexander VI	August 1492 – August 1503
Pius III	September – October 1503
Julius II	November 1503 – February 1513
Leo X	March 1513 – December 1521
Adrian VI	January 1522 – September 1523
Clement VII	November 1523 – September 1534
Paul III	October 1534 – November 1549
Julius III	February 1550 – March 1555
Marcellus II	9–30 April 1555
Paul IV	May 1555 – August 1559
Pius IV	December 1559 – December 1565
Pius V	January 1566 – May 1572
Gregory XIII	May 1572 – April 1585
Sixtus V	April 1585 – August 1590
Urban VII	15–27 September 1590
Gregory XIV	December 1590 – October 1591
Innocent IX	October – December 1591
Clement VIII	January 1592 – March 1605
Leo XI	1–27 April 1605
Paul V	May 1605 – January 1621
Gregory XV	February 1621 – July 1623
Urban VIII	August 1623 – July 1644
Innocent X	September 1644 – January 1655

KEY TERM

Conciliarist A conciliarist is one who believed in the importance of councils of the Church, rather than relying on the view of the Pope.

the **conciliarists** put into action, yet internal divisions within that faction once more returned total power to Rome.

The centre of conciliarist thought was France and successive French kings, from Charles VIII through to Louis XII and Francis I, were only too happy to tap into conciliarist sympathies when it suited their political ambitions in Italy. In 1510, the French quarrel with the

The Catholic Reformation   85

papacy reached new heights, when Julius II dropped France as an ally and vowed to help drive out Louis XII from Italy. In response, Louis summoned a General Council at Pisa in 1511, threatening Julius with deposition. In response, Julius called the **Fifth Lateran Council**, which went through twelve sessions before being dissolved in 1517 by Leo X.

Although the Fifth Lateran had not been summoned with reform in mind, some of the decrees give us an insight into the minds of Catholic reformers. Most of the elites present desired a restoration of past excellence within the Church and an eradication of abuses, yet few were willing to face up to the growing wave of anti-clericalism that was spreading throughout Europe. However, two monks, named Giustiniani and Quirini, produced a more ambitious set of reforms entitled the *Libellus ad Leonem X* (1512), which appealed directly to the Pope to reform the Church. They called for evangelising missions to America, union with eastern Christians, and measures to improve the education and training of the clergy. Yet their ideals were not taken up by Leo X who seemed more interested in theatre and the arts than in spiritual reform.

Effect of the decrees

The decrees of the Fifth Lateran had little effect on the Church, and following Leo X came two largely uninspiring popes in Adrian VI and Clement VII. The pontificate of Clement VII was characterised by chaos and calamity. Under extreme political pressure from both the houses of Habsburg and Valois, Clement had to try to preserve the balance of power in Italy and not forfeit papal power in the process. Unfortunately, an alliance with France resulted in the sack of Rome in 1527, in which an undisciplined imperial army looted the holy city. Moreover, Clement was captured and effectively imprisoned under imperial guard in San Angelo, while Henry VIII continued in vain to attain an annulment of his marriage to Catherine of Aragon (see page 14). Finally, Clement witnessed the rapid expansion of Lutheranism not only in Germany, but also in Scandinavia. Charles V pressurised him to call a General Council but, fearful of its consequences and implications for papal power, Clement held out until his death in 1534.

KEY TERM

Fifth Lateran Council In many ways the reforms proposed by the Council foreshadowed those made at Trent. One of the most significant papal bulls to emerge from the discussions was that prohibiting simony at papal elections. However, overall the proposals made by the Council had little effect on the ground because popes were unwilling to implement them.

His successor was Cardinal Alessandro Farnese, who became Paul III.

Paul III was the most important pope of the Counter Reformation, as it was he who presided over the basis of a Catholic revival. He appointed Fisher, Contarini, Carafa, **Sadoleto**, Pole and Morone as cardinals, oversaw the establishment and development of the Jesuits and Ursulines and, most significantly, called the General Council to Trent in 1545.

The *Consilium*

From the beginning, Paul III was aware of the need to initiate Church reform and, in 1536, he appointed a commission that included Contarini, Carafa and Sadoleto to study this issue. The report was entitled *Consilium delectorum Cardinalium...de Emendanda Ecclesia* (1538). The *Consilium* criticised the system of papal government because it enabled abuses to exist and called for a return of the spiritual leadership of the Pope. Previous popes who had led immoral and worldly lives were criticised, while abuses such as simony and pluralism (see page 10) were also condemned. Greater care and attention was called for in the education and training of the clergy and the scandalous state of monasticism was made apparent, with sweeping reforms called for. Yet, while the *Consilium* demonstrates a new critical attitude within Rome, it was still a relatively unimaginative and traditional document. There was nothing new in identifying the ills and abuses of the Church, and the remedies suggested, such as the tightening up of discipline or more rigorous education for clerics, were not particularly striking in their innovation. Paul III took little notice of the *Consilium*, still believing that a Council of the Church was necessary to implement reform throughout the Church. Luther did take notice of the *Consilium*, as a leaked version soon reached Germany, where it was published in German. The Wittenberg reformer highlighted the self-professed weaknesses of the Church and criticised the Curia for not dealing with central theological issues.

Jacop Sadoleto (1477–1547) Born in Modena, he became Bishop of Carpentias and a member of the commission to study Church reform in 1536, the same year in which Sadoleto was made a cardinal. He helped Contarini draw up the Consilium and later became a close adviser of Paul III.

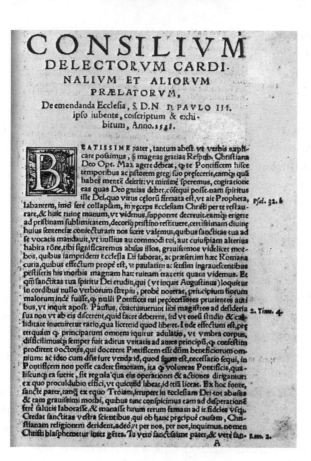

WHY DID PAUL III CALL A GENERAL COUNCIL OF THE CHURCH AT TRENT IN 1545?

On first viewing, Paul III might have seemed little
different from his decadent Renaissance predecessors.
Indeed, shortly after his election in 1534, he made two of
his teenage grandsons cardinals and acquired the Duchy of
Parma for his son Pierluigi. Such blatant nepotism hardly
suggested a pope willing to embrace ideas of reform. Yet
Paul III immediately recognised how desperate the position
of the Catholic Church was in Europe. Not only had
much of Germany become Lutheran by 1535, but England
had also symbolically broken with Rome, and both France
and the Empire were warring once again over the Italian
states. Added to this was the growing threat of the Turkish
Empire. Paul III realised that both in a political and
religious sense he needed to summon a council of the
Church in order to preserve the position and status of the
Catholic Church in Europe.

nepotism

Unlike his immediate predecessors, Paul III was decisive in his decision-making and showed himself willing to confront the major issues. As early as 1536, Paul III summoned a council for Mantua, but was thwarted by the reluctance of France to support a venture that might increase Habsburg strength. Moreover, Paul III was faced with an Emperor who was still pursuing a religious policy of unity through peaceful negotiation with the Protestants.

Regensburg. In 1541, a meeting was engineered by Charles V between leading Protestant representatives and theologians and their Catholic counterparts at Regensburg (see also page 55). The Colloquy of Regensburg was an attempt to find a theological compromise, over 20 years after Lutheranism had emerged as a popular movement. It was doomed to failure; and it is to the credit of those present on both sides, principally Melanchthon and Contarini, that some middle ground was found. Agreement was reached over the first five articles of *The Book of Regensburg* (1541) and, most notably, the issue of justification by faith alone was diluted to suit both delegations in a doctrine entitled double justification. In this, the role of good works was seen as vital in attaining salvation (which satisfied the moderate Catholics present), while the value of good works was gauged by the faith underlying them (which suited the moderate Protestants). Yet there were some issues that could not be compromised over, such as transubstantiation and the real presence of Christ in the Eucharist. Furthermore, both Luther and the Pope recognised that attempts at compromise were futile and that confessional lines in Europe had long been drawn and were now hardened.

Council of Trent. Paul III now prepared the way for a systematic statement of Catholic belief and, in May 1542, he summoned a council to meet in Trent, a town within the Empire but on the Italian side of the Alps, a fact that suited both imperial demands for the meeting to be held in the Empire and papal desires to control proceedings. Yet renewed fighting between Charles and Francis, and then between the Emperor and the Lutheran Schmalkaldic League, foiled the Pope's ambitions.

By 1544, the Peace of Crépy had brought a temporary end to the Habsburg–Valois conflict, while the Schmalkalden League was beginning to fall apart through internal divisions. The military defeat of the Lutherans might force them to attend the Council and abide by its decisions. After more delays, the Council of Trent opened on Sunday 13 December 1545. In attendance, were only 31 bishops and fewer than 50 theologians. Significant individuals included Cardinals **Giovanni Maria del Monte** and Marcello Cervini, along with the Englishman, Cardinal Reginald Pole.

Few could have predicted then that this Council would meet in three periods at Trent over the following eighteen years and focus the attentions of 270 bishops. Of these bishops, 189 were Italian and many of them relied on the papacy for grants and income, which suggests that they may just have been loyalist yes-men ready to support and endorse any papal initiative. Yet there were bishops from Milan, Naples and Venice whom we would not regard as papalists, and any control that successive popes did have over the Council was down to their own character and assertiveness.

WHAT WAS THE ROLE AND IMPORTANCE OF THE COUNCIL OF TRENT?

The Council met in three sessions over an eighteen-year period. The first lasted from December 1545 to March 1547; the second from May 1551 to April 1552 and, after a ten-year lapse, the final session met from January 1562 to December 1563. Decision-making procedure was established at the first meeting. Three papal legates led the Council, with Cardinal del Monte as president. The papal legates drew up the agenda of issues to be discussed, while only bishops and monastic leaders had the right to vote. While votes were taken in the general congregation, small splinter committees often thrashed out contentious issues of reform or theology, and paved the way for agreement. The clerics at Trent were also under pressure from secular princes, who were keen to see that their power was not eroded by any measures of reform.

Cardinal del Monte (1487–1555) Son of a jurist, del Monte studied law at Perugia and Siena before becoming chamberlain to Julius II. He succeeded his uncle as Archbishop of Siponto and became Bishop of Pavia in 1520. A cardinal from 1536, he was co-president of the Council of Trent and became Pope in 1550. A generous patron of the arts and his love for banqueting and hunting hardly suggest that Julius III was interested in reform. He did endorse the second session at Trent in 1551 and he had the satisfaction of returning an England, under Mary Tudor, back into the papal fold, albeit briefly.

Sessions I to VIII

During its first period (sessions I to VIII), the Council was faced with the problem of whether to deal with reform or definition of doctrine. Emperor Charles V wanted disciplinary reform to be dealt with first, so that Protestants could later be invited to the Council and unity over doctrine could be attained. Paul III saw the need to make a confident and thorough statement of Catholic belief in order to reassure the faithful. In the end, it was decided to deal with both issues concurrently, alternating between reform and doctrine.

In terms of doctrine, the Council issued an important decree on the Protestant teaching of scripture alone. The Council agreed that scripture and tradition should have equal validity as sources of truth. It was also re-affirmed that the Church was the sole interpreter of scripture and that the Latin **Vulgate** version of the Bible was free of error. All seven sacraments were upheld as being necessary for salvation, although not all were deemed necessary for

KEY TERM

Vulgate The Vulgate is the main Latin version of the Bible, produced in the late fourth century. For Catholics, it remained the source of authority. Protestants translated the Vulgate into their mother tongue (the vernacular).

SACRO CONCILIO GENERALE DI TRENTO

Incominciata sotto il Pontificato di Paolo III. Regnando l'Imperatore Carlo V. l'Anno 1545. terminata l'Anno 1564. Intervenero 7 Cardinali, 4 Arcivescovi, 7 Prelati, 227 Vescovi, 12 Generali di tutte le Religioni, 12 Dottori e Teologhi, 8 Ambasciatore di Principi.

To cope with increased numbers at the final session of the Council of Trent in 1562–3, an amphitheatre was constructed. The legates and cardinals face the semicircle, with the lay envoys on their left.

The Catholic Reformation   91

every man. The significance of these agreements is that they were essentially conservative in their outlook and merely re-affirmed traditional Catholic teaching. Moreover, such decrees were clearly aimed at defining the Catholic position in relation to Protestantism and deliberately highlighted supposed Lutheran errors.

The most important decree was that of January 1547, which related to justification by faith and took up 16 chapters and 33 canons! Lutheran notions of faith alone or grace alone were repudiated, while a theological middle ground was ploughed by the Catholics, which upheld the idea of man's free will and the value of good works, while also emphasising God's initiative.

By comparison, the reform decrees of 1545–7 were of little significance. Traditional laws prohibiting absenteeism and pluralism were renewed, although they were rarely enforced. Regular preaching was encouraged by the Council and bishops were reminded of their pastoral duties towards their flock. As the delegation prepared itself to discuss the Eucharist, an epidemic of plague broke out in Trent and, as a consequence, Paul III took the decision in March 1547 to transfer the Council to Bologna, in the Papal States. Indeed, Paul had been anxious for some time over the increasing power of Charles V within the Empire and this was the excuse he had been looking for to switch venues. Yet after a crushing victory over the Schmalkaldic League at Mühlberg in April 1547, Charles was in no mood to move the Council to Italy and he ordered his delegation to remain in Trent and continue discussions. Charles was not only defying papal authority but also advocating renewed discussions with the Protestants in order to impose a lasting peace on the empire. Things got worse in September 1547 when the Pope's son, Pierluigi Farnese, was murdered in Milan by the Imperial Ambassador after the former had allied himself with France.

Sessions IX to XIV
There seemed little hope of the Council's meeting again until, in November 1549, Paul III died, to be replaced by Cardinal del Monte as Julius III. The new pope summoned the Council to Trent on 1 May 1551.

Sessions IX to XIV lasted until April 1552 and were notable for the presence of a handful of German Protestant states, including Brandenburg and Saxony. Their presence served only to illustrate the enormous doctrinal gulf that existed between the two faiths and they contributed little to the discussion. Indeed, little progress was made and, once more, the Council was characterised by a conservative outlook. The doctrine of transubstantiation was reaffirmed, while the outlooks of Luther, Calvin and Zwingli were all condemned.

As the Catholic position on the real presence of Christ was defined along with that on Penance and Extreme Unction, a new crisis arose. Charles V had broken the Schmalkaldic League in 1547 with the assistance of Duke Maurice of Saxony who, although Lutheran, had prized the title of Elector of Saxony above any religious loyalty. Charles handed him this title in return for his support but, in 1552, Maurice changed sides again, allied with France, and drove Charles V south into Carinthia. Not only was this a serious reversal for Charles but also for the Council which, fearing invasion, dissolved itself, and the participants fled.

Pope Julius III died in 1555 before the Council could be reconvened and his successor, Marcello Cervini, died after only 20 days in office. In the same year, Charles V's brother, Ferdinand, took over as Emperor and almost immediately agreed upon the Religious Peace of Augsburg with the Lutherans, which legally recognised the existence of Lutheranism in the Empire (see pages 58–9).

In May 1555, the 79-year-old Gian Pietro Carafa became Pope as Paul IV. Anti-conciliar, intolerant and medieval in his outlook on papal authority, he was hardly the man to usher in lasting reform. Added to this was the fact that Paul IV was a Neapolitan and resented Spanish over-lordship of his homeland. The support of the Spanish king, Philip II, was crucial for any council of the Church to meet, yet Paul IV's hatred of the Habsburgs prevented co-operation. Rather than focusing on a council, Paul IV rehabilitated the Inquisition and prosecuted heresy fiercely. On his death in 1559, there was rejoicing in Rome that the reign of terror was over.

Sessions XV to XXV

Paul's successor, Pius IV, saw the need for conciliar reform and, on 18 January 1562, the Council reopened at Trent. Meeting until December 1563 (sessions XV to XXV), the last phase of the Council of Trent was the most important. Reform was first on the agenda and in particular the issue of episcopal residence. Many bishops and cardinals feared any reform in this area since many of them profited from absenteeism and pluralism. Moreover, the question of whether the residence of bishops was obligatory by divine law or ecclesiastical law threatened papal authority. In particular, the Spanish bishops led by the Archbishop of Granada, Pedro Guerrero, advocated that residence was demanded by God's law, and that the papacy should not be permitted to grant dispensations. Behind such moves was a fundamentally nationalist agenda from the Spanish contingent. Although heavily outnumbered by Italian clergy, the Spanish hoped to weaken papal influence in Spain and enhance the identity of Spanish, national Catholicism. Pius was angry when he heard that such a contentious issue had been openly raised without his consultation. Eventually, a compromise was reached that stated that, while a hierarchy existed in the Church, which had been divinely instituted, any bishop elevated by the Pope was legitimate and worthy of that title. A decree also stated that bishops were bound to reside in their dioceses by divine command, although the terminology was left deliberately ambiguous and the role of the papacy was never clearly defined at Trent.

Meanwhile, the Emperor and the French were calling for a legitimisation of communion in both kinds, as practised in the Protestant Church. It was agreed that the decision over whether the laity should take the cup or not should be left to the discretion of the papacy. Therefore in 1564, communion in both kinds was granted to some areas of central Europe by Pius IV after much coercion from the Emperor. In 1584, Gregory XIII withdrew the cup from the laity, remarking that such practice confused the laity.

The other major doctrinal debate concerned the sacrificial nature of the Mass. Responding to Luther's central attacks, the Council decreed that the Mass was truly a sacrifice,

Paul IV. Contemporary engraving.

Pius V. Engraving by Cavallieri, 1588.

KEY PERSON

Giovanni Morone (1509–80) Milanese by birth, he became Bishop of Modena in 1529. A cardinal from 1542, he presided over the Council of Trent as the pope's representative. Imprisoned under Paul IV for suspected heresy between 1557 and 1560, he was declared innocent by Pius IV and directed the final phase at Trent.

KEY TERM

Legate apostolic A papal representative or ambassador.

which must be said in Latin. The office of indulgence seller was abolished, while it was also agreed that each diocese should establish its own seminary for the education of its clergy. The new chief legate, **Cardinal Giovanni Morone**, opposed calls for clerical marriage and limitations on the financial demands of the papacy.

Divisions

As the Council drew to its conclusion, internal divisions within Catholic ranks became visible. On the one side were the Spaniards who still demanded the recognition of episcopal divine right and the weakening of papal supremacy, while on the other stood the loyal Italians. To exacerbate matters, Charles of Guise, Cardinal of Lorraine, arrived with eighteen French bishops, clutching a list of proposed reforms, including the need to use the vernacular and the authorisation of clerical marriage. Fighting broke out on the streets of Trent between rival factions, but Cardinal Morone was able to diffuse the tension with a series of diplomatic measures: first, the Emperor Ferdinand was appeased by papal recognition of his son Maximilian as rightful successor to the Imperial crown; next, Guise was calmed by his appointment as **legate apostolic** in France.

Pius IV wanted to close the Council and pursue reform in Rome without the tiresome interjections of the Spaniards.

The last weeks of the Council saw some important legislation passed quickly, as Pius suffered a stroke and was near death. The bishops rushed through decrees that a new pope might oppose – the **Church Fathers** agreed that: purgatory existed; prayers for the dead were important; veneration of saints was useful.

Essentially, traditional Catholic belief was affirmed, while abuses were confronted and dealt with. The final session was on 4 December 1563, in which all previous decrees of the Council were ratified and confirmed by Pius IV. This was a symbolic act because it implicitly recognised papal primacy. Amid rejoicing and *Te Deum*s, the Council ended.

What was the significance of Trent?

- The Council of Trent succeeded in clearly defining Catholic doctrine, clarifying areas of Catholic teaching for the faithful. Against a backdrop of Protestant expansion, this was critical and in some ways served to hold the Catholic Church together. While much of the doctrinal definitions were reaffirmations of medieval Catholic belief, the attack upon Lutheran heresies was long overdue. Surprisingly, the position of the papacy remained undefined, although few were left in any doubt that theological reconciliation between Protestant and Catholic was impossible.
- In terms of reform, the Council made lasting and significant provisions for the education of the clergy. The establishment of seminaries, combined with the stress laid upon the pastoral role of bishops within the community, was a watershed mark for Catholic reform. On a limited note, the Council did little to involve the laity in their educational provisions and the religious orders that were becoming involved in missionary work and providing much of the impetus for reform were largely ignored. Furthermore, it was clear that the position of the bishop in his diocese had been strengthened by the legislation of Trent.
- The bishop was now solely responsible for ordinations within his diocese and he was instructed to visit the local parishes regularly. Diocesan synods were to be established, through which leading members of the clergy

Church Fathers In the New Testament, the word Father is used to mean a teacher of spiritual things. The bishops who sat in council at Trent are known as 'the Fathers of Trent'.

Te Deum is sung in praise of God.

could meet and discuss issues of reform or doctrine.

- Finally, the three sessions tell us much about the popes who directed proceedings from Rome. Both Paul III and Julius III should be praised for their initiative in calling and, in the latter's case, reviving the Council, and ensuring that papal ratification of any decree was required. Paul IV, on the other hand, deserves his reputation as an intolerant fanatic who did little to further reform. His preoccupation with the Inquisition at the expense of the Council and his war against Philip II were ill-advised and did much damage to the reputation of the papacy. Pius IV was a more attractive figure and the way in which he reacted to European diplomacy and politics displays a shrewd mind. He managed to appease and gain the support of influential figures while still pressing for reform.
- Now that the decrees had been passed it was up to future popes and Church Fathers to ensure their implementation.

To what extent were the decrees of Trent implemented throughout Europe?

Trent was the catalyst for Catholic reform after 1563 and, although the Council left important business such as the production of a Catholic catechism untouched or unfinished, the nature of reform after the closure of Trent was different from that before 1545. Catholic reform after 1563 was more positive and forward-thinking, and much less of an agitated reaction to Protestant success. It should be noted that the decrees from Trent often took years to make any impact on the ground, and there were vast regional variations in the effectiveness of Trent legislation.

One famous example of how the decrees of Trent were successfully implemented was **Carlo Borromeo**, Archbishop of Milan between 1565 and 1584. Borromeo exemplified the role of the new Catholic bishop: visiting local parishes, attending diocesan synods and establishing seminaries for local clergy. The pastoral role of the bishop was epitomised by Borromeo.

In France, by contrast, the Wars of Religion prevented the decrees of Trent from being published and it was left to

KEY PERSON

Carlo Borromeo (1538–84)
The son of Count Gilbert Borromeo and Margaret de Medici (sister of Pius IV), Borromeo benefited from his uncle's becoming Pope in 1559, as he was appointed Secretary of State, Cardinal and Administrator of the Papal States. Borromeo helped reassemble the Council of Trent in 1562 and, as a consequence of his widespread reforms and desire to eradicate clerical abuses, he was canonised in 1610.

The Catholic Reformation   97

each individual bishop to implement them as he saw fit. In Spain, Philip II authorised the decrees while, in the Empire, the decentralised nature of authority meant that some Catholic states were more thorough and enthusiastic in their implementation of reform than others.

What did the papacy do to implement the decrees of Trent?

Most important were the sixteenth-century popes who succeeded Pius IV, namely Pius V, Gregory XIII and Sixtus V. Indeed the powers of the papacy had been enhanced by Trent as it had full power to interpret and implement Tridentine decrees through the Roman Congregation of the Council established in 1564. In that year, a papal Index of Forbidden Books also appeared along with a Tridentine Confession of Faith, which sharply summarised Catholic teaching. Pius IV also commissioned a Catholic catechism, which was duly published in 1566. Under Pius V, in 1568, there was also a new edition of the Breviary, which was prayed daily by every Catholic cleric in major orders. This was followed in 1570 by a Roman Missal that contained the order of Mass as it was to be celebrated throughout the year.

Unquestionably, we can detect a rise in the quality of bishops throughout Catholic Europe after 1563. Bishops who were educated, committed to their flock and open-minded in the adoption of reform prevailed. Diocesan synods played an important part in implementing Tridentine reform on the ground. Procedure was slowed down, however, by the Curia's insistence that all provincial councils should submit their decisions to Rome for approval. A papal bull issued by Sixtus V in 1588 made this a requirement. Moreover, visitations were a crucial means of ensuring uniform and correct implementation of Tridentine reform in the localities. Borromeo was especially vigilant in his inspection of Milanese parishes.

Gregory XIII showed himself willing to compromise some of the agreements made at Trent in order to further reform. In particular, he was ready to make compromises with the princes of the Empire, many of whom were prince bishops anyway. In 1583, Gregory oversaw, and effectively ensured the election of, the unqualified Ernest of Bavaria to the archbishopric of Cologne, which had been under threat from Protestant forces. In doing so, Gregory not only preserved a crucial Catholic archbishopric, but also attracted support from the powerful Bavarian Wittelsbach family. Ernest was a disappointment, but his successor and nephew Ferdinand was not, and reform in northwest Germany was secure. Moreover, Gregory allowed important princes to tax the clergy and administer church property because it was pragmatic to do so. Tridentine idealism over the reform of abuses had to be put to one side in favour of the support of influential figures such as Duke William of Bavaria.

Sixtus V continued the policies of his predecessors with regard to the centralisation of the Church under the Curia. All bishops were expected to visit Rome on a regular basis and report on the condition of their dioceses. More significantly, Sixtus undertook a reform of the Curia in 1588. Ministries were established to deal with the various branches of administration. These ministries were called congregations and a total of fifteen were created to oversee the business of the Papal States. The Congregation of the Inquisition and the Congregation of the Council were responsible for the implementation of Tridentine reform. Resident papal nuncios were also appointed to all important European royal courts and it was their job to ensure that reform was being carried out in the localities.

HOW IMPORTANT WERE THE JESUITS AS AGENTS OF CATHOLIC REFORM?

The Jesuits were perhaps the leading contributors to Catholic regeneration in Europe. They were, in many ways, an example of forward-thinking modernity amid a backdrop of Catholic conservatism. The Jesuits made enormous contributions to Catholic reform as both teachers and missionaries.

Education
Even before the Council of Trent had been summoned, the Jesuits had been heavily involved in education. The

earliest Jesuit colleges appeared in Bologna (1547), Messina (1548) and Palermo (1549). In Rome, Ignatius Loyola founded the Collegium Romanum (1550) and the Collegium Germanicum (1552), which would later act as a training school for catholicising missions to Germany. Up until this point, Jesuit colleges were solely established to train and educate the order. Yet soon, mixed colleges were set up that also included non-Jesuits. When Loyola died in 1556, there were over 30 colleges across Europe and the New World. By 1600 this number had increased to 236 colleges offering instruction and guidance free of charge. Funded by wealthy benefactors and secular princes, the colleges laid out a programme of study that encompassed a classical humanist and Christian education. Boarding was available in most colleges and it was often the case that seminaries were attached also. In time, a Jesuit education took in three phases: college, academy and university. By 1600, European society rated the Jesuit colleges among the finest educational institutions, due to the structured curriculum combined with a strict Christian ethic and rigorous instruction. After Trent, the Jesuit colleges often served as an alternative to diocesan seminaries and, for the Jesuits themselves, the colleges provided a ready supply of recruits for the order. In 1565, the Society of Jesus had 3500 members. By 1626, that figure was 15,500 and growing. Jesuit colleges also trained future secular clergymen, lawyers, princes and the ruling elites of Europe. Emperor Ferdinand II, Duke Maximilian II of Bavaria and Cardinal Richelieu all received a Jesuit education, while most of the royal confessors of Europe were Jesuits and, in that role, they certainly helped to shape policy in France and the Empire. The Jesuits' role in education therefore consolidated Catholic renewal among the upper classes of Europe.

Worldwide mission

The Jesuits had long held an ideal of worldwide mission, which was unconnected to the events at Trent. In 1540, Francis Xavier travelled to India on a Portuguese ship and became the first Jesuit missionary to the non-European world. He reached Goa in 1542, preaching to European settlers there about their Christian duties towards their Asiatic neighbours. Xavier reached Japan in 1549 and founded a Japanese church, which flourished intermittently until it was banned in 1640. News of Xavier's missions was read with great pride back in Rome and epic tales of a 300-mile hike to Kyoto in Japan and missions in far-flung forests and jungles became the stuff of legend.

During the next two centuries, thousands followed Xavier to Japan, to Spanish and Portuguese America, and to the country that was next on Xavier's itinerary before his death in 1552 – China. While thousands were converted in foreign lands, Jesuit missions also had an important role to play in Europe. Preaching tours of the countryside in Italy, Spain and France taught rural folk simple prayers and hymns. Catechism classes were also established and success was seen to have been achieved when all parishioners had recognised their sins. The execution of Fathers **Campion** and Parsons in England in 1580 demonstrates how perilous such missions could be. Furthermore, many missionaries found it difficult to break down local folk belief and superstitions and, in the countryside especially, the understanding of basic Christian doctrine was poor. Even after a mission had been completed, there was no guarantee that the instruction offered would be upheld, and regular visitations in the years following were required.

The Jesuits were in many ways the foot soldiers of Catholic renewal, a fact that the general Ignatius Loyola recognised in his energetic outlook on Counter Reformation Catholicism. More than any other order or institution, the Society of Jesus tapped into the new post-Tridentine atmosphere and environment, working effectively to preserve and expand Catholicism.

HOW IMPORTANT WAS THE INQUISITION IN COMBATING HERESY?

The Inquisition was an ecclesiastical court for the discovery and prosecution of heresy. Generally, the aim of the Inquisition was to make heretics aware of their errors and lead them towards repentance and confession, thus returning them to the Catholic Church. Two principal Inquisitions stand out as being significant during this period.

- The first was the Spanish Inquisition set up by papal authority and with the full backing of Ferdinand and Isabella in 1478.
- The second Inquisition, the Roman, was set up in 1542 by Paul III to counter Protestantism and regulate the publication and censorship of books.

Spanish Inquisition

The initial targets for the Spanish Inquisition were Jews and Muslims. Practising Jews and *conversos*, or New Christians (Jews who had converted to Christianity), were dealt with especially harshly and, between 1481 and 1488, over 700 of them were burned. The Inquisition also served as a useful centralising tool for Ferdinand and Isabella as it had powers to override any other institution. Even Sixtus IV had to back down in 1482 when, on demanding that appeals to the papacy should be allowed by defendants, he was told that the Inquisition was under royal supervision. In the 1540s, the Spanish Inquisition turned to Protestants and *moriscos*. Between 1540 and 1700, the Spanish Inquisition sentenced 50,000 suspects, with the most active anti-Lutheran prosecution being in the outlying areas of Barcelona, Saragossa and Seville. The procedure relied upon denunciations to uncover targets and then examination of the accused by the Inquisition would take place, occasionally using torture. If found guilty, the accused could face a number of punishments, ranging from flogging to death by fire. At the head of the Inquisition was the Inquisitor-General, a post held by Cardinal Ximenes between 1507 and 1517. The crown also placed censorship under the control of the Spanish Inquisition and, in 1545, it issued its own index of forbidden books, with revisions in 1551 and 1559.

Roman Inquisition

The aim behind the Roman Inquisition, in 1542, was to establish a network of courts throughout Catholic Europe, with its centre in Rome. The Inquisition would centralise papal authority and supersede local ecclesiastical courts. Yet as we have seen, Spain already had an Inquisition, as did Portugal, while other states were reluctant to allow such an institution to ride roughshod over traditional privileges and traditions. Even close to home in the Italian states, there were problems enforcing decisions. Nevertheless, decisions made by the Inquisition and the Congregation of Index were seen by Rome to be binding upon the whole Church.

In many ways, the driving force behind the Roman Inquisition was the austere and severe Gian Pietro Carafa, future Paul IV. Carafa had been impressed with the Inquisition of Spain while working in Madrid as a papal nuncio. Carafa, with the support of Ignatius Loyola and Cardinal Juan Alvarez de Toledo, brought pressure to bear on Paul III to revive the medieval papal Inquisition. Given the go-ahead after a cell of Protestants was uncovered in Lucca, Carafa bought a house in Rome and fitted it with prison cells. The Roman Inquisition never functioned on the same scale as its Spanish counterpart. Between 1542 and 1761, there were roughly 100 executions by the Inquisition in Rome. Contrary to subsequent Protestant propaganda, the procedure followed by the Inquisition was careful and respectful with regards to legal rights. Clear proof was required, along with two witnesses and rarely was torture used to extract confessions. Anonymous denunciations were illegal, while a defence lawyer was guaranteed for the suspect. Punishments were generally lenient and designed to bring the guilty party back into the Catholic fold. The public **abjuration** of Protestantism before the parish congregation might often suffice, for example.

The work of the Roman Inquisition did expand inevitably under Paul IV, in 1555. Along with Michele Ghislieri (future Pius V), he oversaw the burning of several Venetian heretics in Rome. Moreover, in 1559, he issued the first official Roman Index of prohibited books: a severe list which even included the works of Erasmus and all translations of vernacular Bibles. While, in the 1520s, 92 works of Erasmus had been published in Italy, none were published during the 1560s. In all, approximately 550 authors were listed, including Machiavelli and Rabelais. In reaction, on news of the death of Paul IV in 1559, the buildings of the Inquisition were plundered and looted. Yet the final sessions of Trent drew up another Index of Forbidden Books and reiterated Paul's line that Catholics were not free to read books by heretics. In 1571, a standing committee of cardinals was established, known as the Congregation of the Index, to deal with printed works.

Therefore, rather than the numbers of those that were executed by the Roman Inquisition, which were relatively small, we should perhaps concentrate on the fear that the institution created in society; a fear which not only drove Italian Protestants into exile, but which also repressed intellectual thought. Biblical culture among the laity was particularly affected by the Index, and the use of the Inquisition as a vehicle for social and spiritual control always left the Church unsure of just how devout and loyal its congregation was.

CONCLUSION: HOW SUCCESSFUL WAS THE CATHOLIC REACTION TO THE CHALLENGE OF PROTESTANTISM?

- The Catholic Reformation was not just a movement against Protestantism. Attempts at reform and regeneration existed before Luther and were, to some extent, continued and given a renewed focus and energy after 1520. Out of the crisis of religious division came many positive aspects for Catholicism.
- The Counter Reformation hardened the confessional divide in Europe, consolidating traditional Catholic territory in Bohemia and Austria, while developing a strong Catholic identity in Poland.
- Southern Germany, under the influence of the Wittelsbachs of Bavaria, became a Catholic stronghold, while France, after the Wars of Religion, witnessed a vibrant surge of Catholic renewal, which increased throughout the seventeenth century.
- Catholic reform made little impact on northern Germany, England or Scandinavia, where political circumstances and popular support allowed Protestantism to flourish.
- The Council of Trent ought to be viewed as a major success for the papacy and Catholicism. Not only did it define Catholic doctrine in a sharper and more conclusive way than ever before, but it also initiated crucial reforms, most notably in the realm of education.

- The extent to which the decrees of Trent were implemented on the ground varied from region to region and state to state. Philip II was the only leading Catholic ruler to accept the decrees of Trent immediately. However, Tridentine reform certainly improved the standard of education and discipline among the higher clergy across Catholic Europe.
- The impact of Tridentine reform could take decades to permeate all levels of society. The emphasis on the pastoral role of the bishop and the need to visit parishioners highlighted how much work had to be done in the localities. The base level of Christianity in the countryside was low.
- Above all else the Jesuits personified Catholic reform and Counter Reformation. Through their soldierly commitment to Loyola's *Spiritual Exercises* they crossed cultural and national borders in their catholicising missions. Jesuit colleges, catechisms and missionary work, both in Europe and overseas, gave an impetus and energy to Catholic reform.

SUMMARY QUESTIONS

1 How extensive was Catholic reform before the Council of Trent?

2 To what extent did the Society of Jesus uphold their oath to 'fight for God in faithful obedience to our most holy lord, the Pope'?

3 List the decrees of the Council of Trent and explain the significance of each.

4 To what extent were the decrees of Trent implemented on the ground?

5 In what ways and with what success did the Catholic Church react to the challenges to its authority during the sixteenth century?

AS ASSESSMENT 1

IN THE STYLE OF EDEXCEL

Unit 2: Luther and the Reformation in Germany, 1517–55
There are two main question types that you will have to answer.

Predominantly descriptive questions

These questions are targeted at the following:

- The process by which something happened.
- The ideas, aims and motives of an individual – in this case, Luther.
- The state of affairs at a certain time – for example, the state of the Catholic Church in 1518.
- A comparison of the ways in which a situation changed.
- The response of individuals or groups of people to a certain situation.

There are a couple of points for you to note:

- It is essential that you note the main point of the question.
- Although the examination board uses the word 'describe', they actually want you to analyse and point out the links between factors.

Questions

Example 1 Describe how Luther's criticisms of the Church differed from those of Erasmus.

Example 2 Describe how Lutheranism survived in Germany 1535–55.

Example 3 How did the views and theology of Luther differ from those of the Catholic Church?

Example 4 How did Charles V attempt to contain the spread of Lutheranism?

The type of questions that ask you to answer the question 'why'?

The key to these questions is for you to argue your point of view and to link factors.

Here are some examples:

Example 5	Why did the controversy over indulgences lead to a split in the Church in Germany?
Example 6	Why did Charles V fail to deal with Lutheranism?
Example 7	Why did Luther's protest lead to a split in the Church in Germany?
Example 8	Why was Martin Luther able to gather and maintain support for his ideas?

To answer these questions you need to include the following:

A line of argument. In answering these or any other question that asks you to analyse, you need to develop an argument that directly answers the question. Your line of argument will end up in your making a judgement in response to the question, which is important if you are to be guaranteed the top marks.

Prioritising. Often, you have to weigh up a variety of factors in analysing a certain issue. As part of your line of argument you should try to prioritise the factors. This means choosing one factor as the most important in relation to the others.

Using evidence. Any line of argument needs to be backed up with evidence that is accurate and detailed. The information you use will make your argument a valid one. Analysis does not work without evidence to back it up.

Complexity. You want your line of argument to be complex. This means that you will be able to show that the issue you are analysing is complex. The way to do this is to complete a plan that includes more than one line of argument.

Interrelation of factors. You should explain in detail how the factors are linked. For example, you should make it clear that you see the relationship between the different causes: how one factor leads to another; how one factor makes another more significant; how some of the short-term causes relate to the long-term causes.

Historical interpretations. Where relevant, it is useful to explain how and why historians differ in their accounts and explanations of what happened.

How to analyse
So far, you have been told what you need to do. The next stage is to understand how you do it. Here are some points of advice:

Planning. The most important step in writing a response to an answer is your plan. **You should never start answering a question without making a plan first.** If you are

answering a question for homework, you should spend a fair amount of time on your plan. Once you have worked out a clear plan, you have answered the question.
A word of warning, however: in an examination, you are advised not to spend too much time on your plan – if you have 30 minutes' writing time you should spend no more than three minutes on your plan.

The plan should include:

- the lines of argument you intend to use
- how you are going to structure your ideas and what you are going to put in each paragraph.

Here is an example of a plan in response to question *Example 7*.

Why did Luther's protest lead to a split in the Church in Germany?

- Once Luther's ideas became clear it was obvious that unity was impossible as his views differed significantly from those of the Church.
- Favourable conditions in Germany, including numerous printing presses and the support of crucial political figures such as Frederick the Wise, turned Luther's academic campaign into a popular protest.
- *Introduction.* The success of your response relies on being able to answer the question directly from the start. Therefore you should use your lines of argument to write the introduction.
- *Paragraph 1.* Argue the importance of the division on the Eucharist and sacraments.
- *Paragraph 2.* Popular support for Luther's ideas meant that compromise was increasingly unlikely.
- *Paragraph 3.* The division between Luther and the Church reflected political divisions in Germany at the time.
- *Conclusion.* Here you briefly reinforce your argument. The conclusion is a useful place in which you can make a sustained judgement.

How to sustain an argument. There are some useful tips to help you sustain an argument. In your answer, use the words in the question throughout your answer – for example, if the question is about 'splits' in the Church, then use the word 'splits' in your answer.

At the start of each paragraph, it is important that you use words/phrases that lead into analysis. Phrases to use include:

- One should argue that…

- It is clear that…
- The most important point to consider is…
- Without doubt the most significant reasons for…
- Essentially…

When writing analytical answers you should avoid starting a paragraph with phrases/statements that will lead you into a narrative answer. These might include:

- In (followed by a date)…
- The following year…

Paragraph structure. This is a suggestion of how you might structure your paragraphs:

- Argue
- Explain
- Detail
- Reiterate

Style. How you write your answers is important. These are extracts from students' answers to the following questions:

This extract is from the introduction. Note how the student is direct in response.

Example 1. Describe how Luther's criticisms of the Church differed from those of Erasmus.

Erasmus and Luther agreed that the Church was in need of reform. They also agreed that the scriptures had been misinterpreted and mistranslated. However, Erasmus argued for reform from within the structures of the Church, whereas Luther's movement challenged the very foundations of Catholicism. As Luther's teachings became more radical, so Erasmus distanced himself from the Wittenberg Reformer.

Below is another example of an introduction. This example is in response to an analytical question. Note how the introduction is more direct and argumentative.

Example 8. Why was Martin Luther able to gather and maintain support for his ideas?

The most important reason why Luther gained popular support was because his message appealed to many in Germany who were discontented with the Church. Linked to this is the fact that Luther adapted his message to suit different audiences. However, it should be stressed that he was helped by a favourable set of circumstances.

Unit 1: The German Reformation 1517–30/Alternative B Unit 1

Read these sources and answer the questions.

Source A The spiritual wolves 1520–1 The first two lines under the picture read 'Look at this strange beast, a wolf clad in churchly dress, rampaging among the sheep; a red hat runs after it, there is the wolf's cousin. Beware, you sheep, run not away from him who hangs on the cross.'

Source B Appeal to the ruling elites, 1520
Every prince, noble and city should strictly forbid their subjects to pay annates to Rome… No secular matter is to be referred to Rome…The far-reaching and fearful oaths which bishops are wrongfully compelled to swear to the Pope should be abolished… Since this example of oppression hinders the bishop from exercising his proper authority… The Pope should exercise no authority over the Emperor… The Pope should withdraw from temporal affairs.

[**Glossary:** Annates are the sum of money paid to Rome on the uptake of a bishopric.]

Source C Adapted from Luther's Ninety-Five Theses, 1517
5 The Pope has neither the will nor the power to remit any penalties beyond those he has imposed either at his own discretion or by canon law.

6 The Pope can remit no guilt, but only declare and confirm that it has been remitted by God; or at most, he can remit it in cases reserved to his discretion. To ignore such remissions would of course leave the guilt untouched.

35 It is not Christian teaching to preach that those who buy off souls or purchase confessional licences have no need to repent of their own sins.

Source D Adapted from *Doctor Martin Luther's Passion*, 1521
This book was written after the Diet of Worms in support of Luther.

Luther answered as a Christian: 'My writings do not concern this world but God…' And [the bishop of] Trier asked 'Are you a follower of evangelical truth and of St Paul?' And Luther answered: 'Thou hast said it. To this I was born, and for this I came into the world, that I should restore to their purity the words of the Gospel and of St Paul, because the papists have distorted them to their own use… to the detriment of the German nation.'

> a Study **Source A**. From this source and your own knowledge, explain the meaning of 'a wolf clad in churchly dress, rampaging among the sheep; a red hat runs after it, there is the wolf's cousin'.

How to answer this question

Style. The key to answering this question is to use information from both the source and your own knowledge. To reach full marks you need to be explicit (state clearly) which information you are getting from the source and which information you are using from your own knowledge.

> b Study **Source B**. How useful is this source as evidence concerning Luther's attitude to the papacy?

Structure. Before answering this question you need to take account of the following points:

- To judge how useful the source is, you must try to work out the positive and negative points to be made about the situation and the purpose of the author.
- You must also compare the usefulness of the source against your own knowledge.
- You are also expected to mention the extent to which the author's views were typical of the period. Another question you should ask is what gaps there are in the evidence.
- The usefulness of a source depends on the questions asked of it. An example of such a question might be: 'Can it be corroborated (backed up) with other evidence?'

c Study **Sources C** and **D**. How far does **Source C** support the views expressed in **Source D**?

The question is asking you to show that you can cross-reference sources and that you can explain the similarities and differences between them. This is how you structure your answer:

Introduction. The answer is that Source C supports the views expressed in Source D to a certain extent.

Similarities. In the next paragraph you need to explain that the sources do agree to an extent. Explain how the sources agree and back up your claim by using brief extracts from the sources.

Differences. To gain full marks it is important that you highlight the differences between the two sources. This you should do in this paragraph.

In both paragraphs make sure that you *explicitly* refer to both sources.

d Study **all** the sources. Using all these sources and your own knowledge, explain how far you agree with the view that Luther's attack on the Catholic Church centred on spiritual rather than political issues.

It is recommended that you spend one-half of the time spent on the assignment in answering Part d.

This is an 'up to a point but' type of question. The question is centred around the nature of Luther's attack on the Catholic Church. To answer this question effectively you need to do the following:

- Plan your lines of argument.
- Ensure that in your answer you use both the sources *and* your own information to back up your argument. This is extremely important. When you check through your answer, make sure that your references to the sources are explicit. It is good practice to quote from the sources, but your quotes should be brief.

PART 2: CROSSING AS/A2 SECTION

The French Wars of Religion and the expansion of Calvinism in France, 1540–1610

INTRODUCTION

This part of the book aims to clarify:

- The expansion and progress of Calvinism in France.
- Opposition to Calvinism in France, including an explanation of the French Wars of Religion.

The assessment section at the end of this part of the book is directed at students completing the AQA unit 3 course essay on the French Wars of Religion. The assessment work for those studying the Edexcel unit 4: Calvin and Calvinism to 1572, can be found on page 169 at the end of the A2 section on Calvinism.

This part of the book attempts to deal with the following questions:

- **Section 1.** How, and with what opposition, did Calvinism grow in France?
- **Section 2.** What are the main features of the French Wars of Religion, 1562–98?

SECTION 1

How, and with what opposition, did Calvinism grow in France?

KEY POINTS

- The lack of strong monarchical leadership throughout most of the second half of the sixteenth century in France allowed Calvinism to emerge as a popular movement, while the noble, aristocratic support the movement attracted gave it the necessary protection and patronage to survive.
- Therefore, both internal and external factors contributed to the expansion of a movement that often developed against a backdrop of violence and turmoil.

Persecution of Calvinists

The roots of French Calvinism lay abroad with Calvin himself, illustrated by the publication and circulation of the French edition of the *Institutes and Ordinances* in 1541. The 1540s did not see expansive growth, but there was certainly an increasing awareness of Calvin and Geneva among French intellectuals and literate merchants. Obviously the French crown perceived Calvin to be a threat to social and religious order for, in 1542, the *Institutes and Ordinances* were banned by Francis I (1515–47) as part of a national clampdown on heretical activity. The policy of attacking Calvinism was continued by Francis' son, Henri II (1547–59). As part of his campaign against heresy, Henri issued the Edict of Chateaubriand in 1551. This reinforced the ban on Calvin's works and ordered searches of bookstalls and towns suspected of smuggling in heretical literature. Henri condemned Geneva as a place of ill fame, and correspondence with the city was forbidden to all Frenchmen on pain of being labelled favourers of heretics. The punishment for such a crime was harsh indeed: imprisonment or a hefty fine.

Exile

The step-up in monarchical persecution forced many French followers of Calvin into exile, including Calvin's successor in Geneva, Theodore Beza. Most headed for Geneva, which numbered 5000 immigrants during the 1550s. The exiles contributed to the development of French Protestantism through an outpouring of evangelical propaganda and missions back to France to spread the word of Calvin. Many of the exiles returned out of the **Genevan Academy** as trained missionaries. Therefore, while it was the duty of the self-titled *Rex Christianissimus*

KEY TERM

Genevan Academy
Established in 1559, the Academy served as a crucial seminary for the training of Calvinist ministers. Many exiles from France trained at the Academy before returning on missions to their homeland.

Map of France during the Wars of Religion, 1562–98.

KEY TERM

Nicodemism
A term deriving from the actions of Nicodemus who came to Jesus by night in order to avoid persecution. Calvin wrote at length about this practice of withholding one's religious conviction out of fear, regarding it as a weak compromise.

(Most Christian King) to uphold Catholicism and stamp out heresy, the actions of Francis and Henri succeeded in creating a strong resistance base in Geneva.

Calvin himself was in close contact with events in France through a network of contacts. He wrote to the growing Calvinist congregation in France in 1544, urging them to declare their faith openly and to stop reading the gospel in secrecy while still openly attending Mass. In short, Calvin was asking his French brethren to abandon the Mass and face charges of heresy or flee the country. This letter of 1544 was addressed to the **Nicodemites** and demonstrates Calvin's conviction that those of the Reformed faith were the Godly; the elect, those chosen by God for salvation. Persecution and martyrdom were symbols of God's favour and should be accepted by the congregation as such. Such a belief may seem rather harsh, and Calvin was certainly asking a lot of his followers, especially as he lived safely in Geneva. Nevertheless we can see, even at this early stage, how the doctrines of predestination and **Divine Providence** gave comfort to Calvinists. In particular, they nurtured a sense of conviction, resistance and inevitable triumph over Catholicism among those of the Reformed faith.

Moves towards a national church

Inevitably, however, large numbers of Calvinists continued to worship secretly for the time being. Open displays of loyalty would mean death, as demonstrated at Meaux in 1545, where fourteen Protestants were burned for having set up a Reformed Church on Calvinist lines. Despite repression, Calvinist numbers continued to grow in France, especially among the urban classes. The literate city elites consisting of lawyers and magistrates formed the bulk of Calvinist support during the 1550s, along with middle-class professionals, such as booksellers or goldsmiths. Such men were integral in the setting up of the socially-outward institutions known as consistories (see pages 141–2) and, by 1555, a Paris Calvinist church had been founded. This was followed in 1559 by the first national synod of the French Reformed Church, also held in Paris, which was attended by representatives of eleven French Calvinist churches and which succeeded in adopting a **Reformed Confession of Faith**. The Synod that met between 25 and 28 May 1559 heralded a rapid expansion of Calvinism in France and also marked the first step towards a national Church. In some ways, the growth was slipping out of Calvin's control as he had actually opposed the calling of the first synod, believing events to be moving too quickly.

Support for the Huguenots

Nevertheless, the Calvinists in France, known as Huguenots, were attracting influential noble support, which would form a key ingredient for future survival. Of the ministers sent from Geneva into France between 1555 and 1562, over one-third were of noble birth. Initial noble families to convert included the Bourbons, most notably Jeanne d'Albret, Queen of Navarre and Louis de Bourbon, Prince of Condé, as well as the Chatillon family, including Gaspard de Coligny. The attraction of Calvinism for such families varied between the zealous commitment of a Coligny to the political pragmatism of an Antoine de Bourbon. The consequences for Calvinism were profound. Support from noble families allowed the movement to spread into the countryside, particularly the southwest, where safety from royal edicts could be assured. Moreover, the very magistrates who were supposed to be enforcing royal edicts against heresy were often Huguenot sympathisers. In Paris, where over 3000 Huguenots had sung psalms on the left bank of the Seine in 1558, a magistrate named Anne du Bourg was arrested and burned for heresy.

Catherine de Medici.

**Catherine de
Medici
(1519–89)**
married Henri of
Orleans, second
son of Francis I,
who would rule as
Henri II. Her
husband persecuted
Protestants
assiduously before
his death in 1559.
His son, Francis II,
lasted barely a year
on the throne
before Catherine
assumed great
importance as
regent for her
minor son
Charles IX in
December 1560.
Catherine's policy
of conciliation and
compromise
towards the
Protestants was
motivated by
political ideals and
a desire to maintain
peace. In the long
run, it might be
argued that her
policies exacerbated
the religious
situation in France
and the war of the
Three Henris in
the 1580s
confirmed her
failure to uphold
the French
monarchy in the
light of the
Catholic League
and the
Huguenots.

An increase in tension under Francis II

The threat to the religious and social order posed by Calvinism was a
clear and present one for the monarchy. The untimely death of Henri II
in 1559 after a jousting accident merely acted to increase the tension.
The fifteen-year-old Francis II succeeded his father and immediately he
came under the control of the fiercely Catholic Guise family. Many
French nobles, including Antoine de Bourbon and his younger brother,
the Prince of Condé, were anxious about the amount of influence passing
into Guise hands. Moreover, the widow of Henri II and mother of
Francis II, **Catherine de Medici**, was also concerned about the future
implications of Guise domination. A group of Protestant nobles endorsed
by Condé, and probably Calvin also, launched a bold bid to free Francis
II from Guise clutches in March 1560. The conspiracy of Amboise failed
and the conspirators were punished. Condé was imprisoned, awaiting
execution, when the second royal death occurred in 1560 – when Francis
II contracted a fatal ear abscess.

Toleration under Catherine de Medici

It is clear that the closer the link between politics and religion, the greater
the potential for conflict. Charles IX succeeded and was immediately
protected under the regency of his mother, Catherine de Medici, who was
determined not to allow her eleven-year-old son to come under Guise
control. Condé was released from prison by a regent Queen Mother who,
although Catholic, wished to maintain order through toleration and
compromise. As politics and religion became intertwined, Antoine de
Bourbon and Coligny were given prominent positions within the realm,
while Medici also tried to reunite the French Church by bringing
together Huguenots and Catholics at Poissy in 1561, in an attempt to
reach a doctrinal compromise. The failure of such an initiative was
unsurprising, but the continuing policies of toleration from Medici would
push France ever closer towards a war of religion. In 1562, an edict of
toleration was granted to the Huguenots allowing worship and preaching
outside towns, while Protestant nobles were allowed to hold services on
their land. Suddenly, despite comprising only 8–10 per cent of the
population, the Huguenots had received major concessions and, to the
vast majority of France who had remained Catholic, this was
unacceptable.

The outbreak of war

The Parlement of Paris was slow and decidedly reluctant to pass such an
edict of toleration, while Francis, Duke of Guise reacted with force.
Having put together a military triumvirate consisting of Montmorency
and St André, Guise fired on unarmed Protestants worshipping at Vassy.
Louis, Prince of Condé raised troops in readiness for conflict and, for the
next three decades, the fate of French Calvinism very much depended
upon the military fortunes of the Huguenots. By the beginning of the

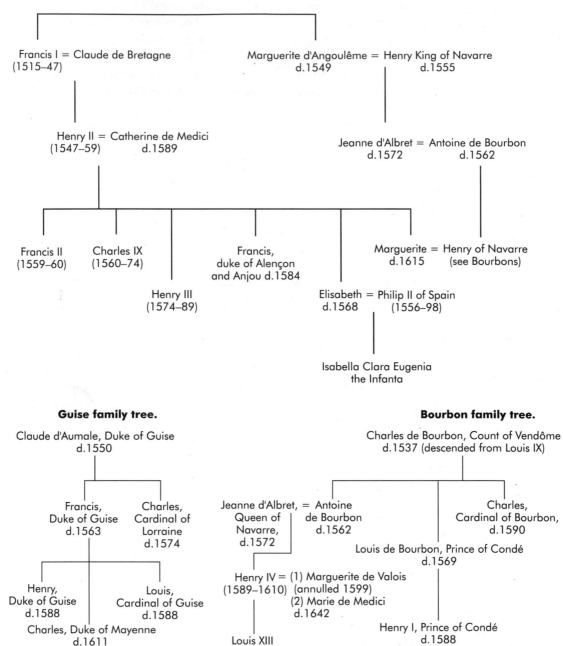

Valois family tree.

Francis I = Claude de Bretagne
(1515–47)

Marguerite d'Angoulême = Henry King of Navarre
d.1549   d.1555

Henry II = Catherine de Medici
(1547–59)   d.1589

Jeanne d'Albret = Antoine de Bourbon
d.1572   d.1562

Francis II
(1559–60)

Charles IX
(1560–74)

Francis,
duke of Alençon
and Anjou d.1584

Marguerite = Henry of Navarre
d.1615   (see Bourbons)

Henry III
(1574–89)

Elisabeth = Philip II of Spain
d.1568   (1556–98)

Isabella Clara Eugenia
the Infanta

Guise family tree.

Claude d'Aumale, Duke of Guise
d.1550

Francis,
Duke of Guise
d.1563

Charles,
Cardinal of
Lorraine
d.1574

Henry,
Duke of Guise
d.1588

Louis,
Cardinal of Guise
d.1588

Charles, Duke of Mayenne
d.1611

Bourbon family tree.

Charles de Bourbon, Count of Vendôme
d.1537 (descended from Louis IX)

Jeanne d'Albret, = Antoine
Queen of   de Bourbon
Navarre,   d.1562
d.1572

Charles,
Cardinal of Bourbon,
d.1590

Louis de Bourbon, Prince of Condé
d.1569

Henry IV = (1) Marguerite de Valois
(1589–1610) (annulled 1599)
              (2) Marie de Medici
              d.1642

Henry I, Prince of Condé
d.1588

Louis XIII
1610–43)

Henry II, Prince of Condé
d.1646

French royal family tree.

French Wars of Religion in April 1562, Coligny himself estimated that there were over 2150 Calvinist churches in France and possibly over 50 per cent of the nobility converted. Although probably slightly optimistic, Calvinism in France had seen a rapid expansion and one that would continue until 1572. Yet despite a basic church framework beginning to appear and a network of synods and consistories emerging, Calvin's hopes of an orderly conversion had been dashed.

HISTORICAL INTERPRETATIONS

To understand fully why Calvinism failed to emerge as the public faith in France over the course of the French Wars of Religion and beyond, we must look to the work of Mack Holt *The French Wars of Religion 1562–1629* (Cambridge, 1995). Holt argues that French society and order was bound together by the **Gallican** principles of one king, one faith and one law. Moreover, the term 'Gallican' reflected the power of the French crown in spiritual affairs and the unique relationship that existed between church and state and crown and pope. By the 1438 Pragmatic Sanction of Bourges, Cathedral chapters were to appoint bishops and abbots free from papal or royal interference. This Gallican ideal was undermined in 1516 when Francis I agreed the Concordat of Bologna with Pope Leo X, which passed the appointment of clerical posts into royal hands. Yet, despite Gallicanism being diluted in 1516, the people of France still took the concept very seriously. Indeed in 1562, on the outbreak of civil war, 90 per cent of the population expected the young king and his regency council to uphold the principles of Gallicanism and adhere to his coronation oath, which included a promise to defend the Church and uphold Catholicism. The failure of successive French kings to achieve this plunged the kingdom into years of monarchical weakness and social unrest.

SECTION 2

What are the main features of the French Wars of Religion, 1562–98?

Who's Who of the French Wars of Religion

Francis, Duke of Alençon and Anjou (1555–84)
Youngest son of Henri II and Catherine de Medici and heir to the throne after the death of Charles IX in 1574, he was a maverick figure who turned over to the Huguenots in 1576 for political reasons. Named sovereign prince of the Netherlands in 1582 and touted as a potential husband for Elizabeth I, his sudden death in 1584 plunged France into chaos as Salic law now decreed Henri of Navarre to be next in line to the throne.

Charles IX (1550–74)
He succeeded his elder brother, Francis II, in 1560 at the age of ten, and came under the regency of his mother Catherine de Medici. Influenced greatly by Coligny, he endorsed his mother's policies of toleration for the Huguenots. He was ultimately responsible for the St Bartholomew's Day massacre, but to what extent is debatable, given his rather weak and feeble character.

Gaspard de Coligny (1519–72)
An aristocratic Huguenot leader from the Chatillon family, as Admiral of France his support and patronage were crucial to the Huguenot cause. He gained military command after the death of Louis de Bourbon in 1569. The failed assassination attempt on his life sparked off the St Bartholomew's Day massacre in 1572, in which he was finished off by Guise.

Louis de Bourbon, Prince of Condé (1530–69)
Antoine de Bourbon was a less-than-convincing Calvinist and ended up fighting for the Royalist forces. His younger brother, Louis, was the opposite, commanding the Huguenot forces in the first three wars until his death at Jarnac in 1569.

Henri de Bourbon, Prince of Condé (1552–88)
He was the son of Louis and played an important part in the regeneration of the Huguenot cause after St Bartholomew's Day.

Henri de Montmorency, Seigneur de Damville (1534–1614)
Royal governor of Languedoc and son of the Catholic Anne de Montmorency, he surprisingly turned over to the Huguenot cause

in 1576, either through local pressure or in opposition to royal policy. He was won back over to the Royalists after the Peace of Monsieur.

Francis, Duke of Guise (1519–63)

Ultra-Catholic and bitterly opposed to any toleration of Calvinism, he sparked off the first religious war in 1562, when he ordered his troops to fire on unarmed Calvinists worshipping inside the town of Vassy. He was assassinated at the siege of Orleans in February 1563. Catholic nobles throughout France signed a vendetta in reaction to his death, swearing to wreak revenge and spill Huguenot blood.

Henri, Duke of Guise (1550–88)

Son of Francis and leader of the militant Catholic faction from 1563, he was heavily involved in St Bartholomew's Day, probably having authorised the assassination attempt on Coligny and he led troops to murder the Huguenot leaders on the 24 August. He headed the revived and powerful Catholic League in 1584 and became a popular Catholic figurehead. He was welcomed as a hero in Paris after the Day of the Barricades in which the king fled the capital. He was murdered on the authority of Henri III in 1588, at Blois.

Henri de Lorraine, third Duke of Guise.

Henri III (1519–89)

He succeeded to the throne in 1574 and continued the moderate religious policies of his mother and brother. He failed to find the resources to deal effectively with the Huguenot threat on the battlefield and, as a consequence, alienated most of the population. He suffered the humiliation of the Peace of Monsieur in 1576 and then the Day of the Barricades in 1588, both of which illustrate the decline in royal authority during his reign. Overshadowed by Guise, he was forced to have him assassinated in 1588. Henri was himself shot by a Jacobin monk named Jacques Clément at St Cloud in August 1589. His death marked the end of Valois rule in France.

Henri III of France.

Henri IV (1553–1610)

Formerly King of Navarre, his wedding of reconciliation to Marguerite de Valois in 1572 provided the backdrop for St Bartholomew's Day. Forced to abjure Calvinism in the wake of the massacre, he escaped from court and led the Huguenot forces with distinction. Abjured again, this time for good, in 1593 in order to be crowned king. His policy of appeasement and ultimate unity restored peace and order to France. He oversaw the Edict of Nantes in 1598, drove the Spaniards off French soil and restored French finances. He was assassinated in 1610.

Henri IV (Henri de Navarre, Henri de Bourbon).

Catherine de Medici (1519–89)

Presented with power as Queen regent for Charles IX, she pursued a policy of religious toleration towards the Huguenots. She held much influence over Henri III, who continued such policies. Inadequate peace settlements ensured further wars. Never far from political intrigue and collusion, she was heavily involved in the decision to murder Huguenot leaders on St Bartholomew's Day.

Anne de Montmorency (1493–1567)
Constable of France and a leading Catholic nobleman, he formed the military triumvirate along with Guise and St André in 1562, which proved to be the backbone of Catholic force in the first war. Captured at Dreux in 1562, he died after the Battle of St Denis in 1567.

Philip II (1527–98)
King of Spain and increasingly involved in the wars after the Treaty of Joinville in 1584 with the Catholic League, he devoted much time and money to the conflict in France at the expense of other pressing priorities, such as the Netherlands. He was ultimately unsuccessful, as he was defeated by Henri IV.

KEY POINTS

- The key issue to contemplate is how far the Wars of Religion were fought over the principles of religion, rather than political concerns.
- Although it is clear that the wars were used to exploit the weaknesses of the Crown and get control of the government, one should not underestimate the continuing importance of religion in this struggle.
- Most obviously, the fortunes of Calvinism rode on the back of the successes or misfortunes of the rebels.
- The wars continued for so long because of the incompatibility of toleration for Calvinism with the determination of many Catholics to crush Calvinism entirely.

The First War
As Louis de Bourbon, Prince of Condé, oversaw the Third National Synod at Orleans in April 1562, the odds seemed to be stacked in favour of the Catholic forces. Yet, through seizing towns in the north, such as Rouen, and throughout the Midi, the Huguenots were able to control major land routes and waterways, making it difficult for the Catholics to engineer a major pitched battle. Moreover, some towns in the north, such as Rouen, were implicitly Calvinist anyway, in that they harboured large numbers of conventicles and even secret churches that were in their infancy. Therefore, Rouen was won over for the Huguenots from within, while other towns, such as Le Havre, were won by force.

After three months, Catherine de Medici was forced to call on the militant Catholic triumvirate, led by Francis, Duke of Guise, in order to halt the run of Huguenot victories. Such a dependency was dangerous for Catherine's regency, as she had been desperate to dilute the power of Guise. In the short term, the move resulted in several Huguenot gains being overturned. In October 1562, Rouen returned to Catholic hands, although Antoine de Bourbon, the King of Navarre who had sided with the Catholics, was killed.

In December, the Catholics won the only major pitched battle at Dreux, although at the cost of their military commander St André. Moreover, Anne de Montmorency was captured by the Calvinists, while Condé was captured by the Catholics. In February 1563, the first civil war closed with the siege of Orleans, at which Francis, Duke of Guise was assassinated. With two out of the three Catholic leaders dead and one held captive it would mean a new set of faces for the second war. There was no shortage of candidates willing to spill Huguenot blood. At the forefront were the brothers of Francis, namely Claude and Charles, along with his son Henri.

TURNING POINT ONE: THE EDICT OF AMBOISE 1563

The Edict of Amboise ended the first civil war, which saw neither side able to defeat the other on the battlefield. As a consequence, the resulting peace was always likely to be one of compromise. The edict allowed Calvinist worship outside specifically named towns, although the nobility were still allowed total freedom of worship on their estates. This concession reflected the growing importance of Reformed nobles, such as Coligny and Condé. The key point here, however, is the fact that such a compromise peace was never likely to hold simply because it had officially recognised Calvinism and granted terms of toleration. Not only were the eight **parlements** reluctant to register such an edict, but the people were unwilling to recognise it and, even as the edict was being issued, the Guise faction were re-arming in preparation for the next conflict. Indeed, as Mack Holt argues, Catherine de Medici had put into action a vicious circle of events that would be replicated over the next 35 years. An unsatisfactory peace settlement had brought a temporary end to a war in which neither side could muster sufficient resources for total victory.

The Second and Third Wars, 1563–72
The years 1563 to 1572 witnessed two further civil conflicts, provoked by the policies of Medici and inadequate royal edicts. The main point to make is that these edicts granted Huguenot toleration, but they were unenforceable. The years 1564–6 were spent by Charles IX and Catherine on a royal progress throughout France, publicising the declaration that Charles IX was now old enough to rule on his own. There is little doubt that, on their travels around France, the royal party would have been

made aware of the unpopularity of the Edict of Amboise. More worrying was the fact that the Guise faction was beginning to dominate the royal council once again and rumours abounded at court that an alliance was being prepared between Spain and the militant Catholic noble faction at court.

The Second Civil War. As the Spanish **Duke of Alva's** army marched through France on its way to the Netherlands in 1566 in order to restore order there, the Calvinists became worried about a Catholic strike. Tensions in the cities increased and many Catholic noblemen had sworn to uphold a vendetta on behalf of the late Francis, Duke of Guise, who had been assassinated during the first civil war. Swearing to the vendetta was recognition that one upheld Catholic values and was prepared to wipe out all Huguenots to avenge the death of Guise. In a time of acute insecurity, Condé and Coligny reacted by trying to snatch Charles from the clutches of the Guises at Meaux. While regional risings in the south around Montpellier were successful, the kidnap attempt failed and the second civil war began. It lasted only six months and involved only one major battle fought at St Denis in November 1567. The Catholic commander Anne de Montmorency was killed in battle.

While the Catholic forces were victorious in battle they were once again unable to inflict a total defeat on the Huguenots. Indeed, as in the first war, the Catholics made little headway in penetrating the Calvinist strongholds in the southwest of France. The Edict of Longjumeau, dated March 1568, reaffirmed Huguenot rights of worship in designated areas outside specific towns. It guaranteed only five months of peace being, as it was, entirely unworkable.

The Third War. The ensuing third civil war, however, lasted for two years. Foreign aid strengthened both sides militarily. This was especially the case for the Huguenots, who received troops from the Netherlands, itself involved in a bitter struggle against Catholic Spain. As the rebels in the Netherlands became identified with Calvinism, the two separate conflicts became intertwined. The Huguenots were also bolstered by German mercenaries supplied by **John of Casimir**, son of the Calvinist elector of the Palatinate, Frederick III. Moreover, the defence of heavily fortified towns made it difficult for the Catholic forces to make use of their superior numbers and, despite winning two major battles at Jarnac in March 1569 and Moncontour in October 1569, the Catholics were unable to gain total victory.

The death of Condé at Jarnac left Coligny in charge and, having regrouped Protestant forces, he was able to orchestrate the first major Huguenot victory of the war at Arnay-le-Duc in June 1570. Therefore, the resulting peace settlement of **St Germain** significantly favoured the Huguenots, allowing for open worship inside specific towns as well as the

HEINEMANN ADVANCED HISTORY

KEY PEOPLE

Duke of Alva (1508–82)
Ferdinand Alvarez de Toledo, Spanish general who arrived in the Netherlands in 1567 to enforce Spanish control. After establishing the Council of Blood which ruthlessly persecuted those involved in the revolt of 1566, Alva proceeded to defeat William of Orange, entering Brussels in triumph in 1568. Recalled to Spain in 1573, he would later command a successful invasion of Portugal in 1581.

John of Casimir
led the German mercenaries provided by his father, the Calvinist Frederick, Elector of the Palatinate.

Treaty of St Germain, 1570 guaranteed the Huguenots four strongholds for a period of two years. The strongholds were La Rochelle, Cognac, Montauban and La Charité.

right to occupy four fortified towns including the adopted capital of French Calvinism, La Rochelle. Perhaps more worrying for the Catholics was the clause offering civil rights and legal equality to Huguenots in France. The idea that a heretic could hold public office only served to heighten the tensions in the towns, especially Paris, where spontaneous outbreaks of mob violence against suspected Huguenots had been common over the previous decade. With Catherine de Medici still pursuing a policy of reconciliation, yet increasingly dependent upon the militant Catholic faction for displays of force during the conflicts due to the weakening state of royal finances, it became clear that significant blood would be spilled in France before a solution could be found.

TURNING POINT TWO: THE ST BARTHOLOMEW'S DAY MASSACRE, 1572

Reasons for the massacre

The 1572 massacre of thousands of Huguenots within Paris and in the localities was prompted by the failed attempt to murder the Huguenot figurehead, Coligny, on 22 August 1572. Only four days earlier, the unlikely wedding of the Calvinist Henri of Navarre to the daughter of Catherine de Medici, Marguerite de Valois, had taken place in the capital. Hundreds of prominent Huguenots had remained in Paris. The attempted assassination of Coligny was probably planned by Henri, Duke of Guise in retaliation for the death of his father, Francis, at Orleans in 1563. Coligny survived the first attempt and remained in Paris, a city that, by this time, was filled with religious tension. Rumours of a Huguenot reprisal attack on Parisian Catholics, and possibly even the king, were rife and, as a consequence, a decision was made by the royal

Painting of St Bartholomew's Day massacres in Paris, 1572, by François Dubois.

council including Catherine, Charles and Guise that the Huguenot leaders should be murdered before they had the chance to act against the council.

The massacre and its implications

In the early hours of 24 August 1572, the King's Guard, led by Guise, went out onto the streets of Paris and proceeded to murder the named targets, including Coligny. However, such bloodletting was always likely to spread to a civilian population tired of what they regarded as toleration of heretics. Over the next three days, a general massacre of Huguenots took place in Paris, carried out by civilians who were convinced they were acting under the orders of God and King. Indeed, the historians Barbara Diefendorf in *Beneath the Cross* (Oxford and New York, 1991), and Natalie Zemon Davies in *Society and Culture in Early Modern France* (Stanford, 1975), have demonstrated how Huguenots were not just killed, but brutally dehumanised in the process. Bodies were stripped and mutilated before being thrown into the Seine as part of a cleansing process. Over 2000 Huguenots were slaughtered in Paris and a further 3000 in the outlying provinces. The implications for French Calvinism were significant as thousands of Calvinists re-converted to Catholicism, convinced that the massacres were a sign of God's displeasure. Others fled into exile, while the committed minority regrouped in the strongholds of the southwest. The expansion of the 1560s was over and now Calvinism depended ever more greatly upon the nobility for support and protection. However, in the short term, many of the nobility (including the influential Condé) were in exile and Navarre had been forced to abjure Calvinism by Charles IX. In the localities, the local nobility re-grouped and re-armed in preparation for the inevitable fourth civil war.

1572–76: A Huguenot recovery?

The Fourth War. The St Bartholomew's Day massacre had an important impact on the fortunes of Calvinism in France. The psychological and material fallout of the massacre meant that the fourth war of religion necessarily took on a different character from the first three. The Huguenots who were left were more militant. As a war aim, they now targeted the very institution of the French monarchy. Moreover, dependence upon English and Dutch aid became even more important for the depleted Calvinist forces. The fourth civil war also continued to highlight the financial weakness of the crown and the inability of Charles to keep an army in the field for long periods of time. Furthermore, as a consequence of the Edict of St Germain, the Huguenots had been allowed to maintain four fortified towns, to which the Catholic forces now attempted to lay siege. La Rochelle withstood the siege and, despite major losses on both sides, a peace settlement was reached at La Rochelle on 2 July 1573. On 8 July 1573, the Edict of Boulogne formally ended the war in favour of the Huguenots. The terms reflected not the war, but the impact of the massacres on the Huguenot community. Huguenot worship was to be allowed only in the private homes of the Huguenots in three towns, including La Rochelle.

In May 1574, Charles IX died of illness, to be succeeded by his younger brother Henri III. He faced a divided kingdom and a Huguenot movement intent on opposing him. His first crisis was to deal with his own younger brother, Francis, Duke of Alençon. Aged 20, Alençon resented his brother's power and desired greater recognition from the king's ministers. Moreover, Alençon was popular. He attracted the support of moderate Catholic intellectuals and Huguenots known as the *politiques*, who wanted peace at all costs. They joined forces by the Confederation of Milhaud to promote their cause. The *politiques* were even prepared to lay aside the issue of religious purity.

In order to advance his position at court, Alençon teamed up with Henri de Bourbon, son of Louis Prince of Condé. He also made an important alliance with Henri de Navarre, who had recently escaped from court in February 1576. With the aid of Henri de Montmorency, son of the former Catholic Anne de Montmorency, and 20,000 mercenaries from John of Casimir, the Huguenot forces numbered over 30,000 men in 1576. Such a formidable force was not really a reflection of Huguenot strength on the ground but rather as a consequence of foreign aid and nobles who wished to back the winning side. Nevertheless, such a show of strength in 1576 was tremendously worrying for Henri III. His main problem was lack of money to raise a significant military force. The war was without major incident. The Huguenots could essentially dictate terms to the powerless king without firing a shot.

TURNING POINT THREE: THE PEACE OF MONSIEUR 1576

Only four years after French Calvinism had been devastated by the Massacre of St Bartholomew's Day, complete freedom of worship in all towns outside Paris was granted by Henri III (1574–89). Calvinist numbers had not expanded beyond the projected 1.5 million of the 1560s, indeed they had decreased. Yet the terms of 1576 were far beyond anything previously experienced by the Calvinists. Huguenots now had the right to build churches everywhere outside Paris and sovereign judges were to be selected from both Catholics and Protestants. Alençon gained a huge cash settlement and recognition as the Duke of Anjou. Despite such major concessions, the age-old problem of how to enforce such an edict upon an unwilling populace remained. Indeed, Henri III himself hated the treaty, but had little choice but to issue it, given the size of the Huguenot army. Again, however, it should be stressed that the peace was not a lasting one. It served to promote the interest of Alençon, but little more.

The Catholics of France were again much disappointed with the settlement. The only parlement to publish the edict was the one in Paris. All others ignored it and there was considerable violence against Huguenots in the country. Near Bordeaux, there was a spontaneous massacre of Huguenots. It was in this atmosphere that the Catholic League was founded. This was a most important event, as the determination of the League not to make any compromise with the Huguenots was to prolong the civil war for another 20 years. The League was founded by the Governor of Péronne, Jean de Humières. He despised the Huguenot leader Mortmorency and, as a result, founded a League to exclude him from his province. The idea of a League soon spread, with Catholics from across France committing themselves to the cause. The League was created with the clear aim of bringing the Guises to the throne. By December 1576, the League had the approval of the papacy and Philip II, King of Spain. Its foundation marks the hardening of Catholic attitudes in France. It also reflected the weakness of the French monarchy. Despite the League's intention to put the Guises on the throne, Henry III also gave the League his backing. However, he had little choice, as the League had quickly come to represent Catholic opinion.

Monarchical authority collapses, 1576–84

In December 1576, the Estates-General met at Blois. The majority of Catholic deputies were influenced by the hard-line views of the League and argued for a return to war and an overturning of the Peace of Monsieur made only the previous May. A moderate faction did exist in the Estates-General, which recognised the strain that taxation was placing upon the populace. Yet, for the moment, the *politiques* group was outnumbered. Henri III was under pressure to inflict total victory upon the Huguenots. His financial position suggested that this would be an impossible task.

A sixth war began in January 1577, but proved as fruitless for Henri as the others had been. The Peace of Bergerac in September 1577 did not go far enough in its repression of Calvinism to satisfy the extreme faction that had emerged out of Blois. While Protestant worship was curtailed to one town in each district, the same problems that had dogged France since 1562 continued to exist. Henri's position was, by this time, becoming more unstable by the day. The Huguenots still mistrusted the monarchy after 1572, while the Catholics of the League were frustrated by Henry's failure to deal with what they perceived as heresy. Moreover, his failure to provide an heir provoked accusations of homosexuality, which further undermined his authority. Added to this was the impact of fifteen years of civil war on the populace. Taxation, billeting and death had provoked peasant unrest, which manifested itself in revolts across Provence, the Vivarais and Dauphiné.

The seventh war was fought in 1580, ending with stalemate at the Treaty of Felix in November 1580. By 1584, things had got worse when King Henri's younger brother, the Duke of Anjou, died. Henri had no children and the law of succession now pointed to Henri of Navarre as next in line for the crown.

1584–93: The Three Henris

At the heart of this social and political turmoil was religion, for as long as Protestantism was tolerated there would be over 90 per cent of the population to oppose it and, if the king was unable or unwilling to take action, then it was inevitable that other groups would do so. The League itself existed not only on an aristocratic level, but also on an urban one, with the so-called **Sixteen** in Paris being the most radical. The fact that the League permeated all classes, and the violent reaction to the king, demonstrate how deeply embedded the principles of religion were in the hearts and minds of the French people. When the Duke of Anjou died in 1584, the potential consequences were worse than most Catholic Frenchmen could contemplate. Technically, the heir to the throne was now the Protestant Henri of Navarre. The response of the Catholic League was predictable; again it proclaimed its support for a king to be chosen by the Guise faction, which again acted to undermine Henri III. The task of defending the Church ought to have been down to Henri III, but his financial prospects were so bleak that this was impossible. The king was helpless when confronted by such a powerful institution. He bowed to it in 1585 through the Treaty of Nemours, which forbade the practice of Protestantism and revoked all previous edicts of toleration. With all sides under arms, a split soon emerged between those Catholics who supported Henri III and those who supported Henri of Guise. A third faction, the Huguenots, supported Henri of Navarre.

The War of the three Henris. When Henri of Guise marched into Paris in May 1588, he was supported by the Sixteen, who erected barricades and took effective control of the city. The following Act of Union once more illustrates the decline in monarchical authority. Henri III had to recognise the authority of the Sixteen in Paris and the Cardinal of Bourbon as heir apparent. In an act of calculated desperation, Henri III decided to strike at the heart of the League. On 23 December 1588, the Duke of Guise was murdered while at the king's apartments in Blois. The following day, as the King was in Mass to celebrate Christmas, the Cardinal of Guise was killed. While satisfaction was achieved, long-term security was threatened. Radical resistance theories emerged, urging violent overthrow of the tyrant, Henri III. The death of Catherine de Medici in 1589 removed the chief conciliator and forced Henri III to ally with Navarre. With their combined forces camped outside Paris, Henri III was assassinated by a Dominican friar named Jacques Clément. The stabbing ended the Valois line and left France more unstable than ever. The new king, Henri of Navarre (or Henri IV), was a Huguenot. Immediately on coming to the throne he was urged by moderate Catholic nobles to convert to Catholicism. Such a move was impossible for Henri, even if he wanted to do so, as it would have angered the Huguenot community in France.

KEY TERM

The Sixteen
Named after the sixteen quartiers of Paris, this institution represented the urban middle classes of Paris and became increasingly radical and anti-establishment between 1588 and 1589.

Henry IV. Henri of Navarre set about consolidating his fragile grasp on the throne. However, he had opponents to deal with. Philip II of Spain claimed the throne of France on behalf of his daughter and sent an army to France under the Duke of Parma. The Catholic League also challenged Henri, and their army was ably led by the Duke of Mayenne. However, the cause of the League was weakened by two key events: first, the League's army was defeated at the Battle of Ivry in March 1590 by Henri; second, in May 1590, the League's candidate for the throne, the Cardinal of Bourbon, died. However, Henri was still not strong enough to take Paris, despite a long siege. In Paris, the Sixteen became more impatient and attempted to take matters into their own hands by proposing a marriage of the King of Spain's daughter with the young Duke of Guise. Those who did not sympathise with them were treated brutally, including the President of the Paris Parlement, who was hanged. The response of the Duke of Mayenne was to return to Paris to restore order. In 1593, Mayenne called the Estates-General and Philip II sent an envoy to persuade the Estates to propose his daughter Isabella as Queen. This caused many members of the Estates a real problem. They objected to the idea of being ruled by a woman, and especially a foreign woman. The issue was resolved by the pragmatism of Henri when, in July 1593, at the same time as sealing his kingship, he expressed his desire to be 'instructed' in the Catholic faith.

TURNING POINT FOUR: THE ABJURATION OF PROTESTANTISM BY HENRI OF NAVARRE (1593) AND THE EDICT OF NANTES (1598)

The decision made by Henri of Navarre in 1593 to give up Calvinism and return to the Catholic fold has often been seen as a rather mercenary one. Supposedly, Navarre uttered the words 'Paris is worth a Mass'. Such a decision cannot have been an easy one for a man who had led the fight for toleration over the past 20 years. Indeed, his decision was based on the need to restore order, peace and unity within a France tired of civil conflict. It seems as if even he recognised that, realistically, a Protestant could not rule France, and because of this there is a *politique* element to his decision.

For the Huguenots, these were strange times, not knowing what to make of their former leader. Having been crowned at Chartres in 1594, the first task of the new king was to bring peace through the defeat of the league and the driving out of Spanish troops from France. Paris submitted to the new king in 1594 while, a year later, the pope recognised Henri as a Catholic. With the power of the League waning and most of war-weary France behind the new king, Henri of Navarre liberated Amiens from Spanish rule in 1595 and laid the way for the Edict of Nantes.

KEY TERM

Politique
Catholics in Paris who rejected the League on the grounds that civil conflict was ruining the state.

Edict of Nantes

The Edict of Nantes in 1598 consisted of 92 Articles, 56 secret articles and 2 royal **brevets**. The main body of the text underlined Catholic principles, restoring the Mass to all parts of the kingdom and restricting Huguenot worship. However, in the two brevets, Henri made concessions to his former faith, granting a large sum of money to pay the salaries of Huguenot pastors and he also granted the Huguenots 200 fortified towns in which troops could be garrisoned. Such concessions were to be only temporary, lasting only eight years, but the fact that, in 1606, the brevets were renewed, shows how committed the minority of Protestants were to their faith. Essentially, Henri IV had created a state within a state, allowing Calvinist communities to consolidate their position around the Midi. The Edict of Nantes would prove to be the basis of the peace, despite the assassination of Henri IV in 1610 and the wars still dragging on in one form or another until 1629. Indeed, the edict stood until 1685, when it was revoked by Louis XIV, prompting the emigration of over 200,000 Huguenots, many of them to England.

CONCLUSION

- One should conclude, therefore, that in terms of expansion and success, Calvinism never really fulfilled the promise of the 1550s and 1560s when, under guidance from Geneva, it seemed as if the Reformed faith would make deep inroads into French society.
- Yet at no time did Calvinists exceed 10 per cent of the population and, while a skeletal framework of national and regional synods was constructed, the notion of a national church was a long way off.
- The fact that the Reformed faith did survive disasters such as St Bartholomew's Day and the formation of the Spanish-backed Catholic League does illustrate the importance of noble protection and the discipline and organisation of a committed minority.
- Yet one might argue that, in France, Calvinism was destined always to be the religion of a minority during this period; that it necessarily had to be given the Gallican principles that bound society together.
- One must recognise the political aspect of the wars and indeed the economic impact of over 40 years of conflict but, above all else, it should be argued that religion provided the basis for the wars.
- The role of religion cannot only be seen at the highest level, shaping the peace settlements and providing the guiding principle for the Catholic League, but also at a popular level, inciting the ordered yet brutal massacres of 1572.

AS ASSESSMENT 2

IN THE STYLE OF AQA: COURSE ESSAY QUESTION

For Module 3, you will be asked to complete a course essay. The main focus of the questions of the course essay is on explanation. Below are examples of the types of questions you might be asked:

- Explain why…
- With what success…?
- Examine the factors…

The course essay title will be sent to your school/college two weeks before you are to write your response under timed conditions. This will give you two weeks to prepare for the writing of the essay. You will be allowed to use notes when writing your essay, so you must try to plan the essay thoroughly in advance.

Before you answer this question you should read Chapter 6 (pages 66–73) and Section 2 (pages 120–131) of this book.

Questions

> **Question 1.** How significant were the Huguenots as a factor in explaining the outbreak of the French Wars of Religion?

How to answer this question.

- The key to a successful course essay is a long and detailed plan.
- Your main points of argument need to be clearly thought through.
- You need to link the main factors together in your plan and throughout your essay.

General points on structure. It is important that you think about how you will structure your answer before you try to tackle the question. You will be able to plan before you write your timed essay. To answer these types of essay questions you need to do the following:

- Read the question carefully and identify what the question is asking you.
- Provide a direct and to-the-point response to the question.
- Before you start to write, plan your answer carefully.

- In your plan, include a list of points that will form the basis of your argument/judgement. Then briefly map out what you plan to put in each paragraph.
- Start your answer with a brief introduction.
- Keep your paragraphs to the point.
- Chose evidence to back up the points you have made and use it in your answers.
- Conclude in such a way that you clearly state the judgement you have made in response to the question.

Plan. You need to plan your essay to avoid simply running through a narrative account of the 1550s. You need, in particular, to identify the points of argument that would allow you to do this.

Content. You must ensure that the content you use covers the 1550s. You should make reference to the following in your essay:

- The rise of Calvinism in France.
- The nobility's protection of Calvinism.
- The power vacuum created by the deaths of Henri II and Francis II.
- The moderating policies of Catherine de Medici.
- The growth of faction at court.

Style. In your answer, you need to be direct and to the point. Your introduction will contain your main points of argument. Here is an example of a direct introduction made in response to the questions above.

> The protection and legitimacy offered to Calvinism in France by the nobility was crucial to its survival and development during the 1550s. However, as the Huguenots became more confident and powerful, tension grew in the towns, as Catholics vented their anger at having to live side by side with heretics. Furthermore, illegal church building, synods and the singing of psalms on the left bank of the Seine built up a Calvinist identity, which further provoked Catholic hatred. In the short term, it was not so much the Huguenots as political circumstance that hastened the arrival of civil war. The power vacuum following the death of Henri II combined with the misgovernment and naïve policies of Catherine de Medici resulted in official toleration for Calvinism and inevitable violence.

Question 2. Why might Catherine of Medici be held responsible for the St Bartholomew's Day Massacre?

How to answer this question. The main point of this question is to test how well you understand the importance of the role of the individual.

Plan. In your plan, you need to identify the main points of argument. Here are some examples.

- Medici must be held responsible in that her policies of peace through reconciliation and tolerance were naïve.
- Such naïve policies should be seen against the background of growing tensions within towns and cities over the toleration for Huguenots.
- These tensions were in part due to the frustration with the Crown's inability to defeat the Huguenots between 1562–70.
- The trigger for massacre was the failed assassination attempt on Coligny, which sparked the decision to murder Huguenot leaders.

Style. You need to be direct in your response throughout. It is important that your course essay gets off to a good start with a direct introduction that answers the question. Here is an example.

> There is little doubt that Catherine de Medici created the tensions that manifested themselves on St Bartholomew's Day. In the short term, the failed attempt on Coligny's life sparked rumours of Huguenot reprisals and led to the 'official' murder of Huguenot leaders. Yet the way in which Parisian citizens took the massacre into their own hands thereafter demonstrates the resentment that had been stored up since 1562 over the policies of Medici.

Further questions

Here are some examples of the types of questions asked on this subject. Try to write plans and introductions to each one of these.

Question 3. Examine the importance of the Conspiracy of Amboise in illustrating the issues that contributed to the outbreak of the French Wars of Religion.

Question 4. Why had Henri III lost the confidence of the Catholic Party by 1589?

Question 5. To what extent did religion provoke and sustain violence in France, 1562–98?

PART 3: A2 SECTION

Calvin and Calvinism to 1572

INTRODUCTION

The importance of Calvin to the Reformation is considerable. Not only did he work to develop the ideas of Luther, but he also brought a social discipline and organisation that had been lacking. The impact of his reforms in Geneva was to reverberate across Europe. Civil war in France and the Netherlands became linked with the development of Calvinism, thus earning it the title of 'the religion of revolutionaries'. The previous chapters have outlined the main features of Calvinism. The aim of these sections of the book is to explain its development in Geneva and its impact across Europe.

- **Section 1.** How successfully did Calvin establish a Reformation in Geneva?

This looks at how Calvin successfully struggled to reform the Church in Geneva against a backdrop of political opposition.

- **Section 2.** How did Calvinism develop in the rest of Europe?

This looks at how Calvinism spread from its centre in Geneva to the rest of Europe, taking in how the faith was adapted and adopted.

SECTION 1

How successfully did Calvin establish a Reformation in Geneva?

KEY POINTS

- Over nearly three decades, Calvin struggled successfully to impose a Reformed Church structure upon the city-state of Geneva. By 1560, Geneva contained a functioning consistory to maintain discipline, a high-quality **Company of Pastors**, an Academy, which also acted as a seminary for foreign ministers, and a ministerially dominated schooling system.
- Above all, the state of Geneva bore the distinctive marks of Calvin's personal reform and tireless energy. Geneva was unique and distinctive in the nature of Church reform that was carried out there and, in particular, the relationship that developed between the Church, city government and society at large.
- Indeed, Calvin's struggle to implement reform based on the *Institutes* and the *Ecclesiastical Ordinances* gave Calvinism many of its distinctive traits.
- Yet one should not only consider the importance of Geneva in the context of Calvin's struggle to mould an ideal Christian commonwealth, but also for the effect that it had upon the course of the Reformation elsewhere in Europe, most noticeably in France, the Netherlands and Scotland.

KEY TERM

The Company of Pastors was made up of the ministers of Geneva, who met regularly to discuss doctrine and aspects of institutional Church reform. On his return in 1541, Calvin was appalled at the degenerate state of the ministry and immediately he gathered around him a trusted group of pastors, the majority of whom were French.

WHAT WAS THE POLITICAL MAKE-UP OF GENEVA IN THE SIXTEENTH CENTURY?

The drift to Protestantism

In 1530, Geneva was a city of 10,000 inhabitants and it had recently seen major political upheaval. Essentially, Geneva was under the authority of the Duke of Savoy and, as such, owed allegiance to him. However, the city was ruled by a prince bishop, giving considerable power to the clergy. To complicate matters further, the city council and citizens themselves regarded Geneva as an imperial free city. Therefore there were three competing factions at work within the city. Moreover, its location within Europe was always likely to prove troublesome. To the west lay France, which regarded Geneva and Savoy as a convenient route into northern Italy, while to the east lay Berne, a state that had converted to Protestantism in 1528 and favoured expansion into the territories of the

Geneva and her neighbours in the mid-sixteenth century.

KEY PERSON

Guillaume Farel (1489–1565)
Having studied in Paris under the French humanist, Lefèvre d'Etaples, Farel became exposed to evangelical thinking at the renowned bishopric of Meaux. He served in Basle, Metz and Strasburg before arriving in Geneva in 1532 to oversee reform there. In 1536, he persuaded Calvin to remain in the city, where they jointly drafted a Confession of Faith. However, political opinion was against them and, while Calvin made for Strasburg, Farel left for Neuchâtel, where he continued to advance the Gospel.

Duke of Savoy. A decade before Calvin arrived, Geneva had allied itself with Berne in a bid for independence. The military support that Berne could offer would be essential, but the great fear was that Berne would look to absorb Geneva and effectively rule it. In 1526, the alliance with Berne resulted in the expulsion from Geneva of the prince bishop, namely Pierre de la Baume. The Duke of Savoy was never able to launch a successful invasion and, gradually, the city's adherence to Protestantism was established, under the guidance of a Frenchman named **Guillaume Farel**. The Mass was suspended in 1535 and, one year later, Calvin entered Geneva almost accidentally, and was persuaded to stay and work with Farel to consolidate the Reformation.

How successfully did Calvin establish a Reformation in Geneva? 137

Power in Geneva

Calvin had entered a city in turmoil, freshly liberated, but still largely dependent upon Berne. Throughout 1535, pro-Savoy, pro-French and pro-Berne supporters engaged in street fighting, while image breaking or iconoclasm was also witnessed. Large numbers of the population, especially the Catholic clergy, had been forced into exile, while the government was unstable. The city government tended to be dominated by the wealthy, established Genevan elite, picked from a number of families. In terms of the decision-making apparatus of the city, greatest power lay with the **Little Council**, which was made up of 24 of the afore-mentioned elite. The Council of Two Hundred also debated important issues and ratified decisions made in the Little Council, a body they elected annually. Therefore, it is clear that, while prominent individuals held great civic power, the number of these individuals was significantly large. In short, individual families could not dominate Genevan politics, and it was even written into the constitution that only one family member could serve on the Little Council at any one time. Agreement on key issues was rare and internal divisions were inevitable. Indeed, Calvin himself fell foul of such internal faction fighting in 1538.

WHY DID CALVIN'S FIRST ATTEMPTS TO REFORM GENEVA FAIL?

Lack of popular support

Calvin's first stay in Geneva lasted only 20 months and was largely an unhappy one. Upon his arrival in 1536, he stated that there was no Reformation, everything was in disorder, thus demonstrating just how difficult his task was going to be. Working in tandem with Guillaume Farel, but with no official title, some progress was made in their bid to gain popular support for reform of the Church. In November 1536, a *Confession of Faith* was accepted by the Little Council, to which all citizens were to swear. Moreover, in January 1537, 21 articles on the Organisation of the Church and its Worship at Geneva were also accepted. Essentially, the Church structure drawn up in the *Ecclesiastical Ordinances* of 1541 was based upon these articles, which stated that Church discipline and the right to excommunicate lay with the ministers, and it was the Council's role to ratify such decisions. Yet, despite encouragement from the Senate and Council, popular support was not forthcoming. Many refused to swear the oath upholding the doctrines and discipline of the Reformed Church. Many objected to having their conscience bound by an oath drawn up by two Frenchmen. Others objected to the seemingly enhanced powers of the Church with regard to discipline. Public opinion was very much against Farel and Calvin, as demonstrated by the taunting and abuse hurled at them by the citizens of Geneva.

> ## KEY INSTITUTION
>
> **Little Council**
> Made up of 24 men who were elected from the Council of Two Hundred, the Little Council directed policy in the city-republic of Geneva.

Rejection

In 1538, political opinion turned against Farel and Calvin, when four new **syndics** were elected. These men were committed to reform, but not on the model Calvin had submitted, which they regarded as oppressive. Instead, they were part of a pro-Berne faction, which wished to adopt similar practices to those carried out in Berne and, in doing so, offer religious unity and conformity. Moreover, their anti-French sentiments made it clear that there was no place for Calvin or Farel in this new political climate. Farel and Calvin made a deliberate point of excommunicating the whole city as a mark of their refusal to accept the new changes. Both were expelled by the Little Council, and Calvin's first stay in Geneva was over. Having briefly stopped over in Basle, Calvin came to rest in Strasburg where he would spend much happier days before returning to Geneva in 1541. Ultimately, Calvin and Farel had become victims of political faction in 1538. Nevertheless, Calvin recognised that, in order to implement such wide-ranging and radical reform in Geneva, he would require a strong and supportive group of ministers, a supportive council and time. Between 1536 and 1538, Calvin was referred to in council records only as 'that Frenchman'; yet, second time around, his impact would be far greater.

WHAT DID CALVIN LEARN FROM HIS PERIOD IN EXILE, 1538–41?

Strasburg

Calvin and Farel soon parted company, the latter settling in Neuchâtel, where he remained until his death in 1565. Calvin accepted an invitation from Martin Bucer to come to Strasburg and teach from the scriptures and oversee the large French exile population there. Calvin spent three very happy years in Strasburg, where he developed his theology, married, and settled as a citizen of the city. The second edition of the *Institutes*, which appeared in 1539, was testament to the time that Calvin spent studying the Bible and reassuring himself that the views he had laid out in Basle in 1536 were correct. Perhaps more importantly, in his role as minister for the exiled French population, Calvin gained crucial experience as a Church leader implementing reform. Strasburg was not caught up in the political faction struggles that had characterised Geneva and, as a consequence, Calvin felt under little pressure. Moreover, these years gave him an opportunity to discuss theology and practical elements of reform, such as the role of a consistory (see pages 141–2) with **Martin Bucer**. Bucer was a German Protestant who tended to steer a middle course between Luther and Zwingli. Deeply respected and particularly admired for his 1529 translation of the Psalms, Bucer believed that Christian unity was still possible and that Catholics and Protestants might be united under one church. Such hopes were of course misguided but, for a while, such idealism was shared by Calvin.

How successfully did Calvin establish a Reformation in Geneva?

Return to Geneva

Nevertheless, by 1540, the volatile political situation in Geneva had changed once more. The pro-Berne faction had negotiated a new settlement, which had given up much of Geneva's outlying territory in return for military protection. There was a public outcry and the pro-French faction in Geneva swept into power. Unconvinced of the present ministers' capabilities, they called on Calvin to return to oversee reform once more. The decision Calvin had to make was not an easy one, but the fact that he did return in 1541 demonstrates that he believed it to be God's will that he finish what he had started. However, this time he was determined to come back on his own terms, and Calvin made it a condition of his return that a reformed Church constitution be accepted by the city council. Calvin's thinking behind this was that he needed to clearly outline what the role and powers of the Church were before he could begin to mould the city around his ideas and doctrine. In other words, he was looking to create a strong power base from which he could promote reform. So it was that Calvin returned to Geneva. Immediately the council looked to take advantage of his expertise as a lawyer in order to draft a new constitution that reflected the new political outlook of the city. Yet Calvin also had in mind a template for Church reform that would integrate aspects of secular and spiritual government and increase the disciplinary powers of the Church.

HOW DID CALVIN LAY THE FOUNDATIONS OF A GODLY COMMUNITY, 1541–6?

Ecclesiastical Ordinances, 1541

Convinced of his godly duty to return to Geneva, Calvin based institutional Church reform around the *Ecclesiastical Ordinances* (1541). Indeed, he made his return conditional upon the council ratifying his Ordinances. The *Ecclesiastical Ordinances* created a civil and religious structure around which Calvin could foster and guide a community of believers. The Ordinances were drawn up in association with the Little Council, and there is evidence to suggest that the first draft giving complete jurisdictional independence to the Church was toned down to give ultimate authority to the magistrates. Four orders of the Church were identified within the Ordinances, namely the pastors, doctors, deacons and elders. All of these orders had clearly defined responsibilities. The pastors were required to meet weekly in order to study the scriptures and discuss the Bible. These weekly meetings were supplemented by the *grabeau*, a meeting designed for mutual and constructive criticism. In time, these were the men who would form the backbone of Calvin's Geneva, the so-called Company of Pastors. They came to consist of twelve ministers, and their role was to encourage and lead their flock within the city, through preaching and administering the sacraments.

Martin Bucer (1491–1555)
Born in Alsace, Bucer became a friar in the Dominican order before coming under the influence of the works of Erasmus while in Heidelberg. The following year, he became interested in the escalating Luther affair, showing some sympathy for the Wittenberg reformer and sharing his ideals on *sola scriptura* and papal primacy. In 1523, Bucer settled in Strasburg where he oversaw the reform movement. He always strove for unity among Protestants and he was dismayed by the disagreements at Marburg in 1529. Nevertheless, although Bucer himself shared the Swiss outlook on the Eucharist, he was delighted with the compromises achieved through the Wittenberg Concord of 1536, which brought the south German towns into the Lutheran fold.

At first Calvin found it very difficult to find trustworthy and trained men for the job and, increasingly, he came to rely upon French refugees. The pastors would also emerge as a crucial factor in the spread of Calvinism, as they trained foreign missionaries who returned to their homeland capable of promoting and nurturing a reformed community. The doctors were to instruct and teach the community true doctrine and ensure that the scriptures were not being misrepresented or misinterpreted. Deacons were to care for the poor and needy and were responsible for the distribution of alms, as well as maintaining the city's General Hospital, established in 1535. Notably, the city government never really gave up control of poor relief to the deacons. Finally, lay elders were to be appointed by the government and were responsible for discipline. Together with the ministers, they were to meet once a week and oversee the ecclesiastical court, known as the consistory.

The importance of the consistory

The role of the consistory in the creation of Calvin's Church should not be underestimated. The consistory was the defining element of the Ordinances and the way in which magistrates and clergy worked in unison to uphold discipline characterised Calvin's Geneva. The consistory was a remarkably intrusive institution, looking in on the lives of ordinary Genevans. In 1546, when it was fully functioning, it was estimated that one-fifteenth of Geneva's population came before it. The idea of a consistory was not entirely original, as there is evidence that Berne had a similar institution. However, the overall jurisdiction and control that the Genevan consistory possessed over its congregation far surpassed any other similar institution. Ultimately, the consistory has come to be viewed as the vehicle for maintaining a harsh and strict **theocracy**. Yet the consistory actually had three functions:

- **Education.** First, it served as an educational organ in ensuring that the entire reformed congregation had a basic understanding of reformed doctrine. Clearly, this was especially important in 1541, when the new church was still in its infancy. Hundreds were brought before the consistory in that year and encouraged to learn the basics; that is, the Lord's Prayer and the Apostles' Creed. Was this an example of a highly prescriptive institution or just one that expected its flock to have a basic grounding in the Christian faith? Through attending sermons and reciting from the catechism that Calvin published in 1537, the congregation, which was largely illiterate, was able to gain an understanding of scripture. The consistory was particularly harsh on those who held on to any aspects of Catholicism and repeat offenders were barred from taking communion.
- **Counselling.** Second, the consistory acted as a counselling service at which family or business problems could be resolved. Consistory sessions often provided the medium through which quarrels could be

peacefully resolved. Most cases of this nature involved man and wife. Ultimately, if it seemed the only option, the consistory would recommend to the council that a divorce be granted. Here was one area in which the Catholic Church would not have been so flexible. However, it ought to be noted that the penalty for adultery was death.

- **Judicial role.** Third, and to many most important, the consistory worked as a judicial court, ensuring that high moral standards were upheld within the city. Sabbath breaking, gambling, disorderly feasting, drinking and other vices were punished by admonishments, imprisonment or excommunication. The Favre family were notoriously up before the consistory for various misdemeanours, so much so that Calvin wrote, 'a new city must be built for them in which they might live apart, unless they were willing to be restrained by us here under the yoke of Christ'. In 1546, at the wedding of Antoine Lect, various high-ranking senators were accused of dancing. Eventually, Amblard Corne, a leading citizen of Geneva who was also a syndic, admitted to the charges brought against him and, in so doing, implicated many others, including the notorious **Ami Perrin**. Corne was severely admonished and deposed from his office until he gave proof of repentance.

WHAT WAS THE SIGNIFICANCE OF THE CONSISTORY?

The consistory was an institution for social help as well as control. Although the consistory was remarkably intrusive, it was also genuinely caring. Calvin viewed it as the crucial instrument through which people could live the kind of life intended by God.

The right of excommunication remained a contentious issue until 1555, and provoked much political opposition to Calvin. The key question was whether power lay with the civil government or with the consistory. The Ordinances left the issue vague but, ultimately, any decision of this nature had to be approved of by the council. In 1555, the council finally confirmed the right of the consistory to excommunicate. The importance of this should not be underestimated in a society where to be excommunicated meant being cast out and isolated.

However, there were limits to the power of the consistory. In the outlying rural parishes of Geneva its influence was diluted and these areas remained ones, in the eyes of Calvin and his followers, of ignorance and misconduct. Even within Geneva the consistory was not all-powerful; for example, the lay authorities still dealt with criminal procedures. However, the consistory is the best example, in Calvin's Geneva, of Church and state working in unison. Indeed, the model of the Genevan consistory paved the way for other Church governing bodies, such as the kirk session in Scotland.

Ami Perrin was Captain-General of the City Militia and leading syndic in 1553. Perrin married into the powerful Favre family, members of which were regularly in front of the consistory. Having originally backed Calvin in 1541, Perrin gradually assumed political leadership of the anti-Calvin Libertine faction. Perrin became outspoken on the issue of excommunication and where the authority lay to implement it. For the Libertines, excommunication was a secular matter and the Calvinists were too strict in their control of social discipline.

WERE CALVIN'S REFORMS POPULAR?

Calvin's problems

KEY PERSON

Pierre Viret (1511–71) was a Swiss reformer who studied theology in Paris before joining Farel in Geneva in 1534. In 1536, he moved to Lausanne, returning to Geneva temporarily in 1541 to usher in the return of Calvin and offer him support. A trusted friend of Calvin, he settled in Geneva as a minister between 1559 and 1561, sharing as they did the similar principles of a Church independent of the state.

Although the Ordinances provided the theoretical framework around which Calvin could build his Church, the situation on the ground was less favourable. Perhaps Calvin's greatest problem in 1541 was the lack of worthy ministers. Calvin found it hard to trust men who had remained in the city after his expulsion in 1538 and, despite a number of vacancies arising in the early 1540s, he found it hard to fill the posts with ministers of quality. The only man he could trust was **Pierre Viret**, and of the others he was moved to write, 'our colleagues are rather a hindrance than a help to us: they are rude and self-conceited, have no zeal, and less learning'. It was not until 1546 that Calvin had jettisoned the weaker links and appointed men, mainly French, whom he could trust. However, Calvin was going to need the faithful Company of Pastors and lay elders whom he had gathered around him, for the following ten years would be ones of political strife and theological opposition. The wedding of Lect in 1546 had, as we have seen, upset the leading families within Geneva and, for many, the moral discipline that the consistory was imposing was too harsh and oppressive. By the end of 1546, a faction had begun to crystallise around Ami Perrin, who held the important post of captain-general and had married into the powerful Favre family. Perrin had regularly appeared before the consistory, and it was well known that he objected to its power. Indeed, it was no surprise that the faction emerging around him became known as the Libertines. The Company of Pastors objected to Perrin and the way in which his youth militia paraded around in brightly coloured silk knee-length trousers, the very opposite to the sobriety of the ministers. Moreover, Calvin's supporters did themselves few favours in 1547 when, having accused Perrin of treasonable correspondence with King Henri II of France, they had to admit to a lack of evidence and restore Perrin to his former position. Perrin would prove to be a thorn in Calvin's side until 1555.

HOW DID CALVIN ULTIMATELY TRIUMPH IN GENEVA?

Years of struggle

In many ways, the years 1547 to 1555 were crucial ones for Calvin in that, while he had constructed the framework of a reformed Church in Geneva, he now had to build upon that structure and consolidate the work being done by the Company of Pastors and in the consistory. Between 1547 and 1555, Calvin would encounter two types of opposition. One was theological: men who fundamentally disagreed with his doctrine and beliefs. The other was political: men who could not tolerate the power that Calvin had attributed to the Church in Geneva, and who found the work of the consistory overbearing and oppressive.

The way in which both forms of opposition were overcome and the ultimate triumph of Calvin in 1555 demonstrates how strong his position in Geneva had become by that time and, in a sense, the triumph allowed Calvinism to develop its distinctive ecclesiological characteristics. Nevertheless, one should not forget that these were years of struggle, faction and strife, when the fate of Calvinism within Geneva was uncertain. Indeed, Calvin's first theological opponent emerged in 1542, namely Sebastian Castellio, a Savoyard (from Savoy) whom Calvin had actually appointed as head of the *collège* in Geneva. Castellio challenged a number of points of scripture but, most contentiously, he denied that the **Song of Songs** was an inspired book of the Old Testament and attributed to Solomon. Instead, Castellio dismissed it as an erotic poem.

Defeat of Bolsec

In 1544, Castellio was driven out of Geneva as a consequence of his continued attacks on the Company of Pastors. Calvin maintained some respect for his former colleague; even attempting to get him a job as a lecturer in Lausanne. However, from his new home in Basle, Castellio continued to criticise the reformed community he had left behind. The defeat of two higher-profile opponents by the names of Jerome Bolsec and Michael Servetus between 1551 and 1553 would serve to underline Calvin's growing reputation as an international reformer and theologian of note. Bolsec was a former monk who challenged Calvin to a set-piece debate over the doctrine of predestination. Bolsec denied that the scriptures endorsed the idea of God electing man for salvation. However, he was no match for the intellectual might and rigour of Calvin who reinforced his core doctrine with repeated references to the epistles of St Paul and St Augustine. Bolsec was expelled by the council in 1551 for fear that his views might cause social unrest and disharmony within the city. Significantly, the council had backed Calvin, not necessarily because those on it shared his theological stance, but because they wished to maintain order and, increasingly, that is what Calvin had come to represent. Moreover, given the unwilting loyalty of the pastors, the council would have found it hard to dismiss Calvin without prompting the immediate resignation of the entire company.

Servetus

In 1553, the most infamous of all theological opponents arrived in Geneva. Michael Servetus was a Spanish theologian who was already fleeing a death sentence for heresy in Vienna where he had resided between 1538 and 1553. Indeed, there is evidence that Servetus and Calvin had been in written contact before 1553. The two men possibly even met in Paris in 1534, and certainly Calvin was aware of the heretical works of Servetus. Essentially, Servetus was an anti-Trinitarian, that is, he did not believe in the **Trinity** and the divinity of Jesus. He had openly flaunted these views, developing them in print through writing

KEY TERMS

The Song of Songs The Song of Songs (or the Song of Solomon) is the first of five scrolls read at Jewish feasts and at Passover. Opposition to canonising the Song of Songs arose in the sixteenth century due to its erotic nature. Defence of the Song of Songs was based around the idea that it presented the rich wonders of human love.

The Trinity encompasses the doctrine of the Christian faith and outlines three issues. There is to be one God; that the Father, the Son and the Spirit is each God; and that the Father, the Son and the Spirit is each a distinct person. Radicals such as Servetus rejected the relationship between Christ and God the Father.

The burning of Michael Servetus, by an unknown artist, taken from *Les Martyrs de la Science*.

KEY THEME

Judgement on Servetus As Theodore Beza, Calvin's successor in Geneva, wrote of the Servetus case 'only one was put to the fire, and who was ever more worthy than that wicked one having for the space of 30 years in so many sundry sorts blasphemed against the Eternity of the Son of God … and having gathered together all the filthy stinks Satan did vomit out against the truth of God'.

De Trinitatis Erroribus (1531) and *Christianismi Restitutio* (1553). The latter work contained a preface offering a stinging rebuke to the vitriolic criticisms made of him by Calvin. Indeed, there is a certain arrogance about Servetus turning up in Geneva to hear Calvin preach and challenge his doctrine. There is little doubt of the contempt in which Servetus was held by Calvin, and it was no surprise that, when he was spotted in Geneva, the ministers instigated his arrest. The council was reluctant to deal harshly with Servetus and initially he was offered the chance to return to Vienna. However, it soon became clear that he was going to have to be dealt with more harshly, once Calvin had deemed Servetus to be a dangerous heretic. The opinions of the Swiss cantons were also called upon and their verdict was unanimous: Servetus was a dangerous heretic and had to be burned as such. **The Servetus affair** has come to be seen as prime evidence of the harsh and intolerant regime overseen by Calvin in Geneva. However, this is simply not so. First, as with the Bolsec case, Servetus was tried in the secular, criminal courts at which Calvin was called as a leading theological witness to evaluate the views of Servetus. Second, the judgement of the Swiss cantons tells us much about international opinion of Servetus. He had already fled death once and was widely regarded as a heretic by men such as the Lutheran reformer Philip

Melanchthon. Had he not been burned in Geneva, he would probably have met the same fate elsewhere in a Lutheran, Zwinglian or Catholic state; it would have made no difference. Calvin himself even tried to have the sentence reduced to one of beheading which, given how long it takes human flesh to burn, was actually most compassionate. The point here is that the burning of Servetus should not be taken as evidence of a harsh theocracy emerging in Geneva.

Out of the defeat of theological opposition come three key points:

- Calvin's reputation as a theologian was upheld and advanced as a consequence of the endorsement offered by the Swiss cantons and other Protestant churches of his views on Bolsec and Servetus.
- Calvin's knowledge and understanding of the scriptures was almost unparalleled. Stark and disciplined he may have been, but intellectually he was first rate and more than a match for the likes of Bolsec and Servetus.
- The council had supported Calvin's judgements due to his persuasive argument, and through fear of religious unrest in the city and the need for religious unity.

WHAT FORM DID SOCIAL AND POLITICAL OPPOSITION TAKE IN GENEVA?

Reasons for opposition

Nevertheless, the very council that had backed Calvin over points of theology was the source of the political opposition that threatened to topple the reformer. Many of the magistrates on the council were increasingly concerned by the increasing influx of French refugees, escaping religious persecution. By 1540, these foreigners accounted for over one-third (3000–4000 refugees) of the population and, as we have already seen, many were prominent figures serving in the Company of Pastors. To some, the French were pretentious, aloof and self-important, basking in their noble heritage, while denying honest Genevans a daily wage. House prices increased and in a period of economic uncertainty it was no surprise that sporadic outbreaks of **xenophobic** violence marked the late 1540s and early 1550s. Yet ultimately, the support of such refugees would be crucial in explaining Calvin's success and their number would tilt the electoral balance decisively in Calvin's favour in 1555.

KEY TERM

Xenophobic is a hatred of foreigners.

The Perrinists

The Perrinists fronted by Ami Perrin, Captain-General of the city militia, formed the most formidable political opposition to Calvin during the years 1547–55 and, in particular, as we have already seen from the Antoine Lect wedding in 1546, these were men who claimed to be

Libertines

Political faction led by Ami Perrin which denounced Calvin's Ordinances and rejected the moral discipline of Calvinism and the overbearing influence of the consistory.

Libertines and who paid only lip service to the authority of the consistory. The question of where the authority lay to excommunicate was one of the central issues for Perrin and his supporters as, for them, such a decision was primarily a secular one. In some ways, Perrin viewed Calvin as a political rival and one way to lessen the reformers' influence would be to question the overbearing authority he had in moral affairs. Perrin made his point in 1553 over Philip Berthellier, a fellow Libertine who had been excommunicated a year earlier along with two others by the consistory for, among other misdemeanours, repeatedly interrupting Calvin's sermons, usually by belching or farting. In 1553, Perrin insisted that Berthellier, after due apologies, be allowed to take communion again. The issue at stake was so important to Calvin that he offered his resignation. The affair dragged on until, ultimately, Perrin was toppled and the magistrates gave way over the right of excommunication.

Baptismal names

Another serious clash between the Libertines and Calvin ensued over baptismal names. Calvin and his followers wanted to rid Geneva of names associated with Catholicism and therefore banned non-scriptural names, such as Emmanuel or Balthasar. Unfortunately, one of the most popular names in Geneva for both boys and girls was Claude, as a consequence of the nearby shrine of St Claude. Claude was one of the names that Calvin wished to eradicate and therefore anyone presenting a child for baptism in the name Claude would be rejected, and instead an alternative name, such as Abraham, suggested. The result was social turmoil and unrest, so much so that a list of acceptable names had to be drawn up in consultation with the council. Such action might be considered as proscriptive, but again Calvin fought his corner and increasingly the pastors and refugees offered a united front.

The end of Perrin

Then, in 1555, the political tide turned in Calvin's favour, when the Perrinists lost the city election, and the new pro-French council acted quickly to consolidate their one-vote majority by opening up the Genevan electorate to include French, bourgeois immigrants. Such a move virtually sealed Perrin's fate, as there was now little chance of him ever returning to power. In a moment of self-destruction, Perrin took part in a drunken riot on 16 May, which culminated in his attempting to seize the black baton, a symbol of political authority in Geneva and held only by the first syndic, a position which he no longer held. Such an act of treason was punishable by death and Perrin fled in disgrace. Calvin's political triumph was complete and now he could cultivate fully the reformed community that had developed during these years of strife, as well as turn his attentions to affairs further afield, particularly in his homeland.

How successfully did Calvin establish a Reformation in Geneva?

WHY WAS CALVIN SUCCESSFUL IN GENEVA 1541–55?

Calvin's success in Geneva was primarily due to his own determination to impose a Reformed Church structure upon the city-state. By 1559, Geneva had a functioning and effective consistory, a learned and energetic Company of Pastors and an Academy that acted as a seminary for potential ministers from abroad. Moreover, Calvin could look upon a city in which Church and State worked together and where the Church held great influence in terms of excommunication and schooling. Therefore, it is not hard to see why Geneva was regarded as a beacon of reformed Protestantism and was described by the Scottish reformer John Knox as 'the perfect city of Christ'.

The importance of the support of the council

Yet one must not forget that Calvin had to struggle for fourteen long years to mould the Genevan community into leading the Christian life that he believed God wished us to lead. Indeed, as we have seen, the opposition Calvin faced was at times significant; therefore, it is important that we think about how he was able to overcome this opposition. Clearly, the support of the council was important in defeating theological opposition. Let us not forget that men such as Bolsec and Servetus were tried in secular courts at which Calvin acted as a witness rather than a prosecutor. Moreover, in both cases, endorsement from the Swiss cantons was forthcoming, thus enhancing Calvin's theological reputation. The council may have objected to elements of Calvinism that impinged upon secular, political power, but they did not deny Calvin's ability as a theologian and as a scholar. This can be seen in 1553, when Perrin raised objections to the excommunication of Berthelier, yet was unwilling to accept Calvin's resignation. Calvin could threaten such radical action, safe in the knowledge that the council did not want to lose their leading reformer entirely and because he had the backing of a strong and unified Company of Pastors.

Support among the French

The growing support that Calvin received during this period from the burgeoning French refugee population was also crucial in consolidating his position. Only one of the ministers on the Company of Pastors was not French and, as time passed, many of the lay elders were also selected from the French population. The unstinting support they offered Calvin after 1546 placed him in a strong position when he fell into dispute with the council, because the latter could not risk civil unrest or the mass resignation of the company. Moreover, as we have seen, the influx of refugees and the alteration in the electoral law allowed Calvin to attain a political hold over the city as well.

The role of the consistory

Finally, while one could look to the role of the consistory and the lay elders in maintaining moral order and heightening the spiritual awareness of the citizens or the Academy and the doctors in providing teaching and doctrinal expertise, one really ought to emphasise the role of Calvin himself in ensuring that his Genevan ministry was a success. During such a period of political uncertainty and faction fighting, Calvin controlled the key means of communication, namely the pulpit. As well as attending Bible classes and reading Calvin's catechism, Genevan citizens could also hear a sermon every day and three times on a Sunday. Calvin himself preached about five times every fortnight, not only concerning himself with matters of scripture, but also with politics, and his great self-belief in what he was trying to achieve was undoubtedly transmitted to the people. Some have come to criticise Calvin's doctrine as being harsh and almost destabilising in a settled community, given the uncertainties of predestination. Yet there appears to be little evidence of this in Geneva and, by 1555, Calvin's sermons were well attended by a community of believers. The control Calvin had over the pulpit in Geneva isolated the political opposition, which had no such forum, while it also allowed him to regularly make contact with the populace and urge them to live a godly life.

Limitations to Calvin's success

Nevertheless, Calvin was not wholly successful during this period in his attempts to shape the Genevan ministry, and one might also argue that Geneva's existence as the leading light of Reformed Protestantism did not long survive the death of Calvin in 1564. Indeed, Calvin did not always have things his own way after 1555, as can be seen by the council's rejection of the reformers' draft legislation in 1557 to impose severer penalties for moral lapses in behaviour. Furthermore, the lay authorities and secular courts remained in charge of criminal prosecution and the council maintained control over poor relief, leaving the deacons rather redundant. Yet even while we might view such examples as illustrating the continuing power of lay authorities within Geneva, it is fair to say that it was the co-operation between secular and clerical bodies within Geneva that was all-important to the success of Calvinism. However, one could say that, while the template of reform outlined in the *Ecclesiastical Ordinances* of 1541 was followed in Geneva, the story was a different one in the outlying provinces, where ignorance and misconduct remained commonplace. Furthermore, by the 1570s, visitors to the Genevan Academy, funded in 1559 by the sale of Perrin's confiscated lands, were no longer so impressed with what it had to offer, and it was evident that moral standards were slipping. Perhaps by this stage it is the progress of Calvinism on an international scale that is most important, and particularly in France and the Netherlands where, in the 1550s, Calvinism had shown signs that it might replicate the faith's success in its homeland Geneva.

TO WHAT EXTENT WAS GENEVA A THEOCRACY?

The idea then that Geneva was under theocratic rule lacks foundation. That said, it is accurate to assert that both Church and State were to be seen as subordinate to the word of God. Moreover, both Church and State had clearly defined functions and, by 1555, it was accepted in Geneva that control over the right to excommunicate lay with the Church and not with the city syndics. Furthermore, the ecclesiastical system under Calvin had developed to the stage where the Church handled its own business and defined the religious duties of its members. Therefore, the Geneva of 1555 was a very different one from that of 1538 when Calvin had gone into exile rather than allow the syndics to decide who should be admitted to the Lord's Supper. However, it is clear that Calvin's Geneva also experienced a close relationship between civic government and the Church. We should not forget that the city council in Geneva continued to approve potential ministers for the Company of Pastors and that elders were chosen from among the magistrates. Similarly, and most importantly, a syndic always attended consistory meetings. For Calvin, this was largely acceptable as he talked of two regiments of God – one spiritual and one political – that ruled over the people. We have already seen, in the case of Servetus, how the government of Geneva took responsibility for upholding heresy laws and keeping religious peace. One should not be too hasty in thinking of Calvin's regime in Geneva as being a theocratic one in which the civil authorities were usurped or dominated by an overbearing ministry. The two elements of Church and State often worked together, with Calvin emphasising that both were to take God as their president and governor and to make decisions without regard to anything except the honour and glory of God in the security and defence of the republic. By 1560, there was little doubt that Calvin had increasing influence over a co-operative city council, typified by the fact that the attending syndic at a consistory meeting did not carry his staff of office in order that temporal power was kept separate from the spiritual, while the Ordinances continued to allow for unprecedented clerical autonomy.

SECTION 2

How did Calvinism develop in the rest of Europe?

INTRODUCTION

- While Lutheranism was confined to the German states and Scandinavia, Calvinism spread throughout Europe in the second half of the sixteenth century, having a profound effect upon kingdoms such as France and Scotland.
- By 1609, Calvinism had established itself as the official public Church in the United Provinces of the Netherlands, Scotland and a number of German states, including the Palatinate.
- A degree of toleration of Calvinists had been reached in France, while inroads in both England and America would also be made in the future.
- Nevertheless, despite this spread of Calvinism across many borders, the number of people who actually converted was generally a small proportion of the total population of the aforementioned states. This fact must lead to a calling into question of the extent of Calvinist success during this period.
- The revolutionary circumstances under which Calvinism established itself in France and the Netherlands shaped the movement as, after early successes in both countries, harsh persecution from Catholic rulers followed, bringing suffering to thousands of the Reformed faith and forcing many more into exile.

The expansion of Calvinism

The expansion of Calvinism in differing states necessarily followed differing courses, yet we can identify a number of common factors. First, the role of Calvin himself was crucial, especially in his native France. An abundance of letters and works were distributed to the Reformed brethren in France and the proximity of Geneva to towns such as Lyon further encouraged the development of the movement. Moreover, the role of Geneva as a haven for French exiles and training centre for Calvinist ministers and preachers moulded French Calvinism in a way distinct to Scotland and the Netherlands. Second, the organisation and discipline of the movement, which had evolved in Geneva, was vital in allowing the Reformed faith to survive during times of stress. Of course, the model of Reformed organisation from the city-state of Geneva could not be adopted by larger territorial states, but the way in which the system was adapted through **synods**, **colloquies** and consistories (see pages 141–2) was vital to the success of Calvinism throughout Europe.

KEY TERMS

Synod A synod was a meeting of representatives from a number of Reformed churches in order that they might discuss points of doctrine or discipline. Synods might exist at a provincial and national level, and they are seen as crucial to the survival and organisation of Calvinism during this period.

Colloquies Informal assemblies of Calvinist ministers and theologians to discuss issues of doctrine.

Another most significant factor to the expansion of Calvinism was the certainty of faith fostered by Calvinist doctrine and belief. This certainty created a mood of determination and resolve among communities under persecution. Again, the point needs to be made that the absence of strong monarchical leadership was to allow Calvinism to spread. Equally important was the support given to the movement by important sections of society.

THE NETHERLANDS

As in France, Calvinism expanded and developed in the Netherlands against a backdrop of violent unrest and under constant threat of repression, never attracting more than 10 per cent of the population. However, unlike in France, Calvinism emerged triumphant as the public church of the **United Provinces** by 1622.

The direct links between the Netherlands and Geneva were limited, with no missionaries actually being sent to the Netherlands during the 1560s. However, earlier persecution during the 1540s had forced many religious non-conformists abroad to stranger churches in London and Emden. Such churches, under the guidance of men such as John à Lasco, were crucial in overseeing the evolution of Calvinism in the Netherlands from the 1560s onwards and developing an international network of contacts. Bibles and catechisms were printed in these foreign havens, along with Dutch translations of Calvin's work. In 1544, Calvin's letter to the Nicodemites, urging those under persecution to come out from beneath the cross was published along with a translation of the *Institutes* in 1560. By 1554, an organised Reformed Church had been established in Antwerp, and it was in the prosperous, urbanised and educated southern Netherlands that Protestantism began to make serious inroads. By this stage, the basis of heresy prosecution was the *Perpetual Edict* (1550), drawn up by Charles V to uphold Catholicism in the seventeen provinces of his Netherlandish territories. By 1565, the 'Bloody Edict', as it was termed, was becoming increasingly resented, both at a popular level and at a political one. Merchants feared that such a harsh policy was damaging trade links with other Protestant states, while local government officials and the nobility disliked the impingement such legislation made on local privileges and laws. Yet Charles' son and successor, Philip II, was in no mood to dilute the heresy laws, as he demonstrated with the *Letters from the Segovia Woods* in 1565 calling for the relentless application of all existing heresy edicts. In December 1565, a group of lesser nobles formed a league, known as the Compromise of the Nobility, designed to oppose existing heresy laws and the use of the Inquisition in the Netherlands and, in so doing, defend their own privileges and traditions. News of this stance quickly spread to Reformed churches abroad and many Calvinists returned home, buoyed by the news that the Regent, **Margaret of Parma**

United Provinces
The Netherlands consisted of seventeen provinces which, for the first half of the sixteenth century, were under Spanish rule, although each province guarded its liberties and privileges fiercely. The seven northern provinces that made up the Union of Utrecht in 1579 were those that resisted Spanish domination and fought to attain freedom. These provinces in the north, centred around Holland, were known as the United Provinces, and Calvinism became their public faith. By the beginning of the seventeenth century, the United Provinces had emerged victorious and matured into the Dutch Republic.

Margaret of Parma (1522–86)

Illegitimate daughter of Charles V, Margaret married the Duke of Parma in 1537. She became governess-general of the Netherlands in 1559 and soon encountered problems with the Dutch nobility who were anxious to guard their rights. In 1564, she was forced to lose Cardinal Granvelle, her chief adviser, as the nobility felt that, through schemes to expand the number of bishoprics, he was impinging upon their power. In 1566, she appeared helpless in the face of Calvinist advances and expansion and Philip II had to send out the Duke of Alva to restore order. Margaret was furious, believing herself well capable of dealing with Orange, Egmont and Hornes. She asked to be relieved of her duties and, although she returned in 1579, she did not take on a governing role again, leaving the Netherlands in 1583.

(half-sister of Philip II), had been forced to suspend all heresy laws in the face of such opposition. When a Synod of Calvinist Churches met in Antwerp in 1566 and encouraged all of the Reformed faith to come out into the open, central government appeared powerless to prevent Calvinism spreading rapidly throughout the Netherlands.

The Wonderyear, 1566. The returning exiles from London and East Friesland included a significant number of ministers who soon began preaching in the open alongside those who, up until this point, had operated underground. Such open-air evangelism, known as 'hedge preaching', began in Antwerp, but soon spread rapidly throughout the south in the spring and early summer of 1566. Modest crowds of 2000 soon swelled to 5000 by June and an incredible 25,000 gathered outside Antwerp in July to hear the Gospel. Similar meetings took place outside city walls in Tournai, Ghent and Valenciennes, although the religious convictions of the audience are not certain. Some were undoubtedly committed Calvinists, yet many were moderate Protestants with little knowledge of Calvinist doctrine, while others were simply curious of such a large gathering. As the summer progressed and the Catholic authorities looked ever helpless in the face of such demonstrations, more radical activity was encouraged by some of the preachers. At Steenvoorde on 10 August 1566, Sebastian Matte incited his congregation to enter the local monastery and smash the images or false gods within. Such acts of iconoclasm were repeated on a larger and more violent scale in Antwerp and Holland. Calvinism had entered the cities in a dramatic and radical fashion.

Iconoclasts at work.

How did Calvinism develop in the rest of Europe?   153

Reasons for iconoclasm. Just who was to blame for the orderly destruction of 1566 is difficult to assess. The iconoclasts were often encouraged by preachers, as at Steenvoorde, but it was also the case that local leaders and consistory elders led the image breaking. In the short term, such radicalism forced Margaret of Parma to concede freedom of worship to the Calvinists wherever preaching had already taken place. The serious business of organising churches now began, and soon the terms of the Accord were already being broken as Calvinist churches were constructed. In the longer term, the iconoclasm of 1566 was a turning point in the spread of Dutch Calvinism, as many moderate supporters were shocked by the scale and intensity of the violence and moved back towards Catholicism as a consequence. The nobility also recognised that events had got out of hand and they began to re-affirm their allegiance to the regent. By asserting itself in such a radical fashion, Calvinism had lost the silent majority and, with such an infant Church structure in place, the withstanding of a Catholic backlash was going to be difficult. While Calvinist churches openly conducted weddings, baptisms and communion in the Reformed manner, Margaret of Parma collected her military resources and, by March 1567, both Tournai and Valenciennes had been occupied. Throughout 1567, Protestant churches were shut down and over 7000 sought exile in Emden and Norwich. The arrival of the Duke of Alva in 1567 heralded six years of harsh repression in which 1100 death sentences were proclaimed by the Council of Troubles. In scenes that would be replicated after St Bartholomew's Day, 1572 in France, mass re-conversions took place, with over 14,000 abjuring Calvinism in Antwerp alone. The year of wonders had been the high watermark for Dutch Calvinism and, after 1567, the priority was once more survival. Foreign churches were again crucial in this process, with Emden being a prime example. In 1571, a synod at Emden put forward a Reformed Church structure consisting of consistories, classes (designed to train ministers and pressurise civil authorities), as well as provincial and national synods, which might be implemented in times of freedom. Doctrinally, the Dutch Confession of Faith was re-affirmed, yet repression, lack of finances and a lack of ministers made progress slow over the coming years. More importantly, after the Sea Beggars captured Briel in April 1572 (see page 159), the fate of Calvinism depended upon the military fortunes of the Dutch rebels, led by William of Orange.

The significance of William of Orange (1533–84)

As sovereign prince of Orange, William became a courtier of Charles V and stadholder of Holland, Zeeland and Utrecht in 1559. Although raised a Lutheran, Orange became Catholic while serving the King of Spain, Philip II. In 1563, he supported the claims and privileges of the Dutch nobles, forcing Philip to withdraw his leading minister, Cardinal Granvelle. In the aftermath of the 1566 revolt, Orange sought exile in Germany, despite the fact that he had reiterated his loyalty to the Crown.

Portrait of William of Orange aged 22, by Antonio Moro.

He was wise to do so in light of the fate of Egmont and Hornes, which was execution. In 1568, he led an abortive invasion of the Netherlands, which fell flat due to a lack of popular support. In 1572, a more successful revolution was initiated against the Habsburgs, leading to Orange's high point of success – the Pacification of Ghent (1576) in which all seventeen provinces were united against Spain. However, the alliance was short-lived and the following north–south divide, epitomised by the unions of Utrecht and Arras, was regarded as a disaster for Orange. Above all else, he craved religious toleration and conciliation. The events of 1579 suggested that this was not going to be possible. He continued to support the northern provinces, advocating the idea of French support in the form of the Duke of Anjou. In 1584, Orange was assassinated, leaving the United Provinces leaderless and seemingly at the mercy of the Duke of Parma. Religiously, Orange had converted to Calvinism in 1573, in order to identify with the Dutch cause and keep alive the one issue that Philip II of Spain would never compromise on, namely religion. Orange is remembered as the father of the Dutch Republic.

THE DUTCH REVOLT AND OPPOSITION TO CALVINISM, 1572–1609

As with the French Wars of Religion, the purpose here is to discuss the progress made by Calvinism during these years, but obviously religion becomes inextricably linked with politics and, as we have seen already, religion proved to be the catalyst for violence, if not the main motive.

The origins of the Second Revolt, 1567–72

The Dutch Revolt can be seen through a series of crucial turning points, which explain why the Dutch rebels of the United Provinces were able to declare independence from Spain and secure Calvinism as the state religion. In the wake of the first revolt of 1566, Philip had sent the Duke with 10,000 Spanish and Italian troops to restore royal authority. Margaret resented Alva's presence and resigned shortly after his arrival in 1567. Alva took over as governor-general and embarked on a severe and intolerant period of rule, which alienated sections of the Dutch nobility and created tensions that led to a second revolt. A Council of Troubles was established to try those implicated in the first revolt. Over 12,000 were tried and over 1500 executed, including Counts Egmont and Hornes, the two grandees who, along with Orange, had resented Spanish infringement on traditional Dutch liberties. Their execution was unpopular and further demonstrated overriding Spanish influence on noble privilege. The fear created by the Council of Blood, as it became known, probably explains the lack of support for William of Orange's invasion in 1568, which ended in failure. Yet Alva's policies to centralise the Netherlands from his base in Brussels and make them financially

self-sufficient proved disastrous. New taxes named the Hundredth and Tenth Pennies were introduced, which proved extremely unpopular and provided the environment for revolt. The Hundredth Penny proposed a one-off tax of 1 per cent on all capital, a figure agreed on by the estates and collected successfully. The Tenth Penny, however, was a 10 per cent tax on the sale of movable goods and was intended to be a permanent tax. Designed to exploit the wealth of the nobility and infringing on the rights of the States, it was never likely to be popular. A temporary grant from the States appeased Alva until 1571, when he decided to collect the Tenth Penny by force. With Philip engaged against the Turk and few military resources in the Netherlands, this was a bad time to court discontent, and it presented William of Orange with his second chance to launch a rebellion.

The Dutch Revolt: timeline of events

1555	Charles V hands over authority of the Netherlands to his son Philip II.
1559	Margaret of Parma is appointed Regent of the Netherlands.
1561	Philip orders a reform of the ecclesiastical system in the Netherlands, specifically fourteen new bishoprics.
1564	Discontent with the new scheme and grandee resentment of Spanish impingement upon Dutch traditions leads to the dismissal of the head of the Royal Council in the Netherlands, namely Antoine Perrenot de Granvelle.
1565	Philip II's *Letters from the Segovia Woods* reinforce heresy legislation and offer no change in the powers of the council of state.
1566	The Wonderyear sees an outpouring of Calvinist sentiments and iconoclasm. Margaret forced to make an Accord with the nobility and Calvinists, which soon breaks down.
1567	First Revolt fails. The Duke of Alva restores order through the Council of Troubles, which finds 9000 guilty people between 1567 and 1576; two grandees, Hornes and Egmont, are executed.
1568	Orange condemned *in absentia* by the Council.
1569	States-General refuses the imposition of Alva's new tax, the Tenth Penny.
1572	Tenth Penny imposed through force.
1572	Sea Beggars seize Brill and Flushing, followed by several towns in Holland and Zeeland. William of Orange proclaimed stadholder, or governor, of Holland, Zeeland and Utrecht. Mechelen and Naarden sacked by Alva. Orange flees to Holland.
1573	Alva captures Haarlem, but fails thereafter to restore royal rule in Holland and Zeeland. Alva recalled to Madrid and replaced by Don Luis de Requesens.
1573–74	Alkmaar and Leiden flooded to avoid capture by the Spanish.
1575	Philip II declares bankruptcy.
1576	Death of Requesens. Replaced by Don John of Austria. Spanish troops sack Antwerp, destroying 1000 houses and killing 8000 people. Pacification of Ghent agreed between the States-General and Holland and Zeeland unifies the rebel provinces with those formerly loyal to Spanish rule. Both are now committed to driving out the Spanish mutineers. Outbreak of Third Revolt.
1577	Don John signs the Perpetual Edict, with the States-General agreeing to the dismissal of Spanish troops, in return for recognition as governor-general and the upholding of Catholicism.

1578	Calvinist excesses in southern towns such as Oudenaarde, Kortrijk, Hulst, Bruges and Ieper, as well as Artois, alienates Catholic leaders in the south.
	Duke of Parma becomes Regent.
1579	Union of Arras signed by the Catholic, southern provinces of Hainault, Walloon Flanders and Artois, recognising the rule of Philip II and Parma.
	Union of Utrecht signed by the rebel provinces of the north, principally Holland, Zeeland, Friesland, Gelderland and Utrecht.
	Parma's re-conquest of lost territory begins with the capture of Maastricht.
1581	Duke of Anjou becomes Prince and Lord of the Netherlands.
	An Act of Abjuration passed by the States deposes Philip II.
	Orange, having been outlawed by Philip II issues his Apology, which justifies resistance to Philip II.
1584	Orange assassinated.
	Parma's re-conquest continues with the capture of Ghent.
1585	Parma captures Antwerp.
	The Treaty of Nonsuch is signed between Elizabeth I of England and the Dutch rebels sending money and 7000 men along with the Earl of Leicester, as governor-general.
	Johan van Oldenbarnevelt appointed Advocate of Holland.
1587	Count Maurice of Nassau, second son of William of Orange, assumes control of the States' Army.
1588	Leicester resigns.
	Parma ordered by Philip to join the Armada against England.
1590	Parma forced to intervene in France against Henri IV. Spanish forces diluted and royal finances weakened.
	United Provinces declared a Republic.
1592	Parma dies. Two rival commanders succeed him, namely the Count of Fuentes and the Count of Mansfelt.
1594	Maurice captures Groningen.
1596	Treaty of Greenwich signed between the rebels and France and England, recognising the independence of the northern provinces.
1598	Beginning of the rule of the Archdukes Albert and Isabella after the death of Philip II.
1600	Maurice defeated at Nieuwpoort.
	Henri IV invades Savoy, breaking the Spanish Road, which linked the Netherlands with Spanish Italy.
1604	Spinola captures Ostend.
1606	Spanish forces cross Ijssel line.
1609	Truce of Antwerp to last twelve years and Spain recognises the sovereignty of the United Provinces.

KEY TERM

Sea Beggars The term dates back to 1566, when the lesser nobility presented Margaret of Parma with the Compromise that asked for religious toleration. An adviser of the Regent, named Berlaymont, told Margaret not to worry about these beggars. The leader of the lesser nobility, Brederode, took the term to heart and used it as a title to be proud of. Drab, grey uniforms were worn by the honest Dutch beggars and badges with begging bowls became the latest fashion in Antwerp. Therefore, the Sea Beggars of 1572 were coining a title used by the rebels of 1566.

Turning point one: the Revolt of 1572

The capture of Briel by the **Sea Beggars** (effectively pirates in exile from the Netherlands) allowed William of Orange to launch an assault on the northern Netherlands, centring on Holland and Zeeland, where he had been stadholder and where support for him was strongest. Denied of French support after the St Bartholomew's Day Massacre and set back by the consequent recapture of Mons by Alva, the revolt seemed to have failed. However, once established in Holland and Zeeland, it soon became clear that the Spanish would have great difficulty in dislodging Orange. Geography, the lack of Spanish finances and the resentment and resilience stoked by Alva's harsh sacking of Zutphen and Mechelen, all played a part in Dutch resistance, as did religion. William of Orange himself became a Calvinist in 1573, recognising the need to court Huguenot support and that of the Calvinist leaders in the Netherlands. Moreover, the Sea Beggars were committed Calvinists and not only did they give Orange the vital foothold in the north that he needed in 1572, but they also harnessed local fanatical Calvinist support, which ensured that city gates would be opened before them. Indeed, such radical behaviour forced Orange to bring the Beggars into line for fear of alienating town magistrates. Perhaps most importantly, the revolt of 1572 demonstrates that Philip II would never compromise over matters of religion. Much discontent over taxation had arisen in the years leading up to 1572, with the infamous Tenth Penny creating the environment for revolution, yet it was the issue of religion that could not be covered over by the Spanish. The overbearing Catholicism at the expense of Dutch liberties and privileges was much resented, and Orange's calls for religious toleration were echoed throughout the north.

The Revolt survives, 1573–6. In 1573, Catholic worship was forbidden in Holland, while the States of Holland agreed to recognise Orange as Stadholder or governor for Holland, Zeeland and Utrecht. As Alva slowly overcame the rebels, Spanish finances ran dry. Siege warfare proved expensive and, in July 1573, Spanish troops mutinied and then refused to attack Alkmaar. Moreover, the Dutch rebels used the geography of Holland and Zeeland to their advantage, flooding the fields around Alkmaar (1573) and Leiden (1574) to prevent their capture. The 'great bog of Europe', as the Netherlands was known, consisted of a network of rivers and lakes, which made the movement of men and supplies very difficult for opposing armies. Don Luis de Requesens took over from Alva in December 1573 as governor-general, but a lack of communication with Madrid, coupled with financial insolvency, allowed Orange to consolidate his position in the northwest. Peace talks were held with the rebels in 1575, but the issue of religion provided a major obstacle over which Philip would never compromise.

Turning point two: the Pacification of Ghent, 1576

By 1575, Philip II was forced to declare bankruptcy, scuppering Requesen's plans to attack the rebel provinces. With no pay or food, the Spanish troops violently looted and plundered their way through Brabant and Flanders, culminating in the Spanish Fury of 4 November 1576, in which 8000 people were killed. The sacking of one of Europe's greatest cities brought together the rebel provinces and those in the south in agreement that the Spanish enemy must be driven off Dutch soil. Public Protestantism was to be allowed in Holland and Zeeland, and the government was placed in the hands of the States-General. On the back of the Pacification, the Calvinists in the south once more began to come out into the open. A Reformed church emerged from underground in Ghent, aided by a new and compliant city council. By the summer of 1578, Catholic worship had ceased altogether in Ghent, while in Antwerp and Brussels the Reformed faith witnessed similar growth. Yet it was such radicalism, especially in the south, that alienated the southern nobility and compromised Orange's chances of achieving a lasting peace settlement. Traditional liberties seemed just as much under threat by the radical purging of town councils by the Calvinists as they did from Philip. The Duke of Aerschot had even been arrested in Ghent for opposing Orange, and such activity endangered the revolt, while pro-Calvinist committees had forcefully overthrown Catholic magistrates in several prominent southern towns, such as Kotrijk. The confidence of the Calvinists was typified by the aggressive National Synod at Dordrecht in June 1578, which presented a petition to the States-General demanding freedom of worship for Calvinists wherever 100 Reformed families existed. The alliance between north and south was breaking up and at the heart of the split was religion. Catholic leaders in the south reacted to Calvinist assertiveness and radicalism by preparing for confrontation. Such divisions were exploited by Philip and his new governor-general, Alexander Farnese. In 1578, Alexander Farnese restored the three southern provinces of Hainaut, Artois and Walloon Flanders to Spanish control through the Union of Arras, with the promise that foreign troops would be removed and the Catholic religion would be upheld. In response, the northern territories of Holland, Zeeland, Utrecht, Friesland and Gelderland signed the Union of Utrecht. The Reformed congregations of the north were swelled by southern Calvinists who chose to migrate after the break-up of the Pacification of Ghent. Perhaps as many as 150,000 entered Holland from towns such as Antwerp, Ghent and Bruges.

International context and Spanish failure, 1579–1609. The Netherlands was now divided between royalist Catholic south and rebellious Calvinist north. Farnese, later Duke of Parma, continued his re-conquest, capturing Maastricht and Mechelen in 1579, offering generous terms of surrender to towns that had already been starved to the brink of collapse.

In July 1581, the northern rebellious provinces symbolically deposed Philip II as head of state, thus confirming a political situation that had long been established in practice. In his place, the Duke of Anjou was appointed as sovereign prince of the Netherlands in 1582. Anjou was heir to the French throne and was a Catholic. Yet religious loyalties played second fiddle to political considerations as the French were reluctant to miss out on an opportunity to aid the Dutch rebels and thereby disrupt Spanish expansion elsewhere. As it was, Anjou did not last long in his role as sovereign prince, as he resented the checks on his power and authority. He had no authority over the Dutch army and he had no right to convoke the States-General. He returned home in disgrace in 1583 having attempted to seize Antwerp by force. Such treachery made the rebellious provinces wary of foreign figureheads but, in the light of Parma's re-conquest and the assassination of William of Orange in 1584, they recognised that foreign aid was crucial. In August 1585, Elizabeth I signed the Treaty of Nonsuch, which supplied the rebels with 4000 troops and 600,000 florins. The Earl of Leicester became Lieutenant-General and England was to control Flushing and Brill until all expenses had been paid back.

English aid offered a crucial psychological and material lift for the rebels. Leicester's period of government was disastrous, however, as he introduced new taxes that impinged on local privileges and two of his commanders betrayed Deventer and a fort at Zutphen to the Spanish in 1587. Leicester was discredited and his failure in the Netherlands was completed by Elizabeth's demand for English troops to be brought home in May 1588 to defend the coastline. Nevertheless, England now played perhaps an even more important role for the Dutch rebels in 1588 by diverting Spanish attention away from the Netherlands. The defeat of the Spanish Armada was a huge blow to the prestige of Philip II and it was also an expensive failure.

Parma now stopped winning in the Netherlands, as the failure of the siege of Bergen op Zoom in November 1588 demonstrates. In 1589, Spanish troops mutinied again and, between that year and 1607, they would mutiny another 40 times due to lack of pay. Philip was, by this time, heavily involved in the French Wars of Religion, having signed the Treaty of Joinville with the Duke of Guise in 1584, as well as fighting the Turk in the Mediterranean and protecting New World acquisitions. In short, the Netherlands was not Philip's top priority in the 1590s and there is little doubt that this aided the military commander of the United Provinces, namely Maurice of Nassau. For example, Parma himself was commanding troops in France for periods of 1590 and 1591, which gave the rebels a chance to re-conquer territory. Breda, Zutphen, Nijmegen and Hulst all fell to Maurice in these years; successes that would have been unthinkable in the 1580s.

Peace was still also out of the question (due to Philip's intolerance of Calvinism), despite the contrary pleas of Parma who in 1589 recognised that total victory was unlikely. Parma himself was frustrated by his dual roles and indeed Philip was losing faith in him. Parma would have been relieved of his duties had he not been killed in 1592 at Arras. Just how valuable he had actually been was highlighted by the chaos that ensued over his succession. The Count of Fuentes was sent from Spain as Commander in Chief, yet Count Mansfelt claimed authority as Parma's ex-deputy in Brussels. Neither would recognise the other and contradictory commands did little to help the Spanish cause. Spanish involvement in France continued to bring little reward and indeed the nature and focus of the war changed after Henri of Navarre abjured Calvinism and became a Catholic in 1593. Most of France accepted him as Henri IV and rallied around a national war against Spain. In 1596, a Triple Alliance was formed between France, England and the United Provinces against Spain. In 1596, Philip declared bankruptcy for a third time with debts of around 100,000,000 ducats.

Turning point three: the Twelve-Year Truce, 1609

Although the independence of the seven United Provinces was not officially recognised until 1648, the Twelve-Year Truce of 1609 effectively marks the end of the revolt. Various factors contributed to the survival of the Dutch rebels during the years 1579–1609, such as the military acumen of Maurice of Nassau (son of William of Orange); foreign aid from France and England, including the blocking of the Spanish road by Henri IV in 1600, which prevented Spanish supplies from Italy reaching the southern Netherlands; the political skill of Oldenbarnevelt on the States of Holland; along with numerous Spanish bankruptcies. However, the aim here is to study the consequences of the revolt on religion. By the end of the revolt, the United Provinces were openly Calvinist, despite the fact that only 10 per cent of the population of Holland belonged to the Calvinist Church. In towns such as Leiden, Delft and Dordrecht the figure was higher, yet progress was slow due to the continuing shortage of ministers, the high moral and doctrinal standards demanded of Calvinist members, and the competition from other Protestant groups such as Anabaptists and Lutherans. Yet despite being a minority church, the Calvinists were in a strong position, given their organisation and discipline, as well as their contribution to Dutch triumph. Despite facing a serious threat from the Arminian Remonstrance of 1617, which opposed the harsh discipline of Calvinism and the doctrine of predestination, the Calvinist Church survived, its position secured by the National Synod of 1619 at Dordrecht.

Opposition to Calvinism in the Netherlands was severe, in the sense that Philip II never considered a policy of toleration and moderation. He was an ultra-Catholic ruler who wished to maintain religious and political unity in the Netherlands. Just how powerful Calvinism may have become in the Netherlands is hard to gauge, but the events of 1566 suggest that large numbers were interested in Reformed ideas and practices. Yet after Alva's backlash, Calvinism never reached such heights and indeed, in 1576, the re-emergence of more radical elements alienated influential southern nobility. Calvinism survived, however, and played an important unifying role for the United Provinces. As the official state religion of the north it also gave the rebellious provinces an identity and prevented peace negotiations from taking place. The success of Calvinism depended on the military success of the rebels, as it held little popular support after 1566. Opposition was overcome on the battlefield and, by 1609, Calvinism had emerged as the state religion of the United Provinces.

SCOTLAND

After an abortive Lutheran Reformation at the start of the sixteenth century, Calvinism entered Scotland on the back of anti-French sentiment. Mary of Guise had been Regent of Scotland since 1554, in the name of her young daughter Mary Queen of Scots. In 1557, the Protestant lords of Scotland signed a bond of mutual assistance in advancing the Reformation at the expense of the Regent Council. The self-styled Lords of the Congregation (the Earl of Argyll, his son, Glencairn, and Morton) found little support at first, although the death of the Catholic Queen Mary Tudor and the accession of the Protestant Elizabeth gave hope to the Lords and others who were tired of French interference. The fact that Mary Queen of Scots began to style herself Queen of England on account of her descent from Margaret Tudor and the perceived illegitimacy of Elizabeth's mother, namely Anne Boleyn, further enraged the new English queen. On 2 May 1559 **John Knox**, the Calvinist reformer who had resided in Geneva for some time, as well as serving less pleasurable moments on a galley ship, arrived in the Edinburgh port of Leith.

Shortly, Perth declared itself in favour of the Reformation, as preachers such as Methven, Christison, Harlaw and Willock joined Knox in promoting the Gospel and preaching against the idolatry of the Mass and image worship. By May, the Congregation, supplemented by additional Lords such as Ochiltree, Boyd and Monteith, had raised an army and Perth fell to them while St Andrews, Ayr and Dundee all embraced reform. In 1559, Edinburgh fell twice to the Congregation before being recaptured by Guise. Eventually, in 1560, English troops helped the Congregation seize Edinburgh and the death of Mary of Guise in June 1560 in Edinburgh Castle made a political settlement possible. Under the resulting Treaty of Edinburgh in 1560, made between France and England, French troops were to leave Scotland, while an amnesty was

How did Calvinism develop in the rest of Europe?   163

to be granted to those who had opposed Guise. Moreover, a **free Parliament** was to be held in Scotland to settle the affairs of the kingdom and a council was to be chosen partly by Francis II, husband of Mary Queen of Scots, and partly by the Estates of the Realm. The Scottish civil war was over and the way was clear for the official adoption of Protestantism.

The Parliament met in August 1560 and, over the course of four days, the Reformed ministers presented a Scots Confession of Faith, which was duly accepted, and, on 24 August, Parliament abolished the Mass and all papal jurisdiction. Preaching, administration of the two sacraments, and discipline were stressed as the foundations of a true Reformed Church, reflecting the influence of Geneva upon men such as Knox. Such influence was further witnessed just days after the dissolution of Parliament when Knox and four other ministers set about drawing up a plan of ecclesiastical government and organisation that mirrored Calvin's Ordinances. The *First Book of Discipline* identified four office-bearers of the Church, namely Ministers, Doctors, Elders and Deacons. Kirk sessions were also established, highlighting the importance of the consistory.

Yet the political landscape once more changed in December 1560 with the death of Francis II, leaving Mary Queen of Scots to return from France as monarch. Knox described her arrival in 1561 with despair, stating that the sun was not seen to shine for two days: a clear forewarning from God of the impious nature of Mary. Yet pragmatically and sensibly Mary did not try to overturn the Reformation, and instead allowed Protestant worship to proceed as long as she could attend her own Mass. Moreover, the General Assembly of the newly Reformed church could go about its business free from monarchical intervention.

A free Parliament
This was the main part of a separate 'Accord' between the French and the Scots. Free from French Catholic intervention, this parliament would put an end to the Church of Rome as the national Church of Scotland.

John Knox preaching before the Lords of the Congregation. Detail from a painting by Sir David Wilkie.

Of course, Mary's reign was on the whole to be short-lived and disappointing given her inability to choose either suitable political allies or husbands, leading to her execution in 1587 at the hands of Elizabeth. Further years of civil conflict and short-lasting regencies ensued, while James VI approached his age of majority. When he did become king, James saw his appointment as a godly one and he set about restoring the episcopate in which royally appointed bishops would oversee church government. The second generation of Reformed clergy was much opposed to such an idea and, in 1581, Andrew Melville had his *Second Book of Discipline* passed by the General Assembly. The Second Book was important because in it were outlined plans for the creation of district elderships, known as presbyteries, to oversee discipline and the training of the clergy.

GERMANY

Although Calvinism was adopted by 28 states of the Empire, they were generally small and insignificant ones, apart from the Palatinate. While Lutheranism remained the Protestantism of Germany amid an effective Catholic Counter Reformation, **Frederick III** (1559–76), a leading and influential prince, converted to Calvinism. Frederik embraced the Reformed outlook on the Lord's Supper which, through the Consensus Tigurinus of 1549, saw Calvinist and Zwinglian views concur on the Eucharist. Frederick then set about dismissing all Lutheran pastors and replacing them with Calvinist ones. What really appealed to Frederick about Calvinism were the security and discipline and cohesion that the faith engendered. The capital of the Palatinate, Heidelberg, developed into a refuge for exiled Calvinists, as well as an intellectual centre pouring out works such as the *Heidelberg Catechism* (1563). Yet in many ways Frederick's Calvinism was detached from that of Geneva. The Elector recognised the political power and recognition that could be attained through the adoption of Calvinism and the Ecclesiastical Council permeated all levels of Church government and organisation superseding the consistory. The Council was State run and the Elector's physician, Thomas Erastus, developed a political theory that gave Church supremacy to the head of State. Frederick also enjoyed his enhanced importance abroad, offering invaluable aid to French Huguenots and Dutch rebels, and betrothing his youngest son John Casimir to Elizabeth, daughter of the Duke of Saxony. Yet Calvinism in the Rhine Palatinate did not outlive Frederick and Calvinism continued to lack popular backing in Germany.

CONCLUSION: A RELIGION OF REVOLUTIONARIES?

The spread of Calvinism in the second half of the sixteenth century has often been linked with revolutionary activity and one can see why, given the years of strife and religious division in both France and the Netherlands. Moreover, it would be hard to ignore the role of religion in the origins and continuation of both the Dutch Revolt and the French Wars of Religion. Significantly, Calvinism emerged as a movement capable of withstanding repression and instilling in its supporters a self-belief that was not easily tempered. Certainly, the social organisation and discipline that was adapted from Calvin's template in Geneva was crucial to the survival of Calvinism amid fierce Catholic persecution, as were the international contacts that were established between Reformed communities, creating centres of refuge in places such as Heidelberg or Emden.

One can only admire the structure of Reformed churches in the United Provinces and the Midi of France, which allowed the conflict to continue against the odds. Payment of troops and ministers, along with the maintenance of religious discipline, charity and the drafting of Confessions of Faith, emerged from a synodal system that gave the movement both flexibility and strength. Furthermore, even in the worst of times, synods could meet abroad, such as in Emden in 1571 to discuss matters of faith and consolidate a paramilitary organisation. At Emden, solidarity between the Netherlands and France was explicitly demonstrated when the Dutch Reformed gathering subscribed to both the Belgic and Gallic Confessions. Under intense persecution, Calvinism could go underground quickly, with adherents worshipping in small cells or conventicles, which were difficult for the authorities to detect and, even when they did, such cells comprised only eight or nine people. Such conventicles perhaps defied Calvin's criticisms of Nicodemism, but the longer such cells survived the stronger the movement became, as we have seen in France where, by 1562, there were over 2000 churches.

This then raises another important point, which is that, while Calvinism had to adapt to revolutionary circumstances, one should not underestimate its popular appeal in France and the Netherlands during the 1560s. Calvinism emerged from years of conflict in both countries as a minority faith, but in both it seemed at one stage as if Calvinism would sweep all before it. Successful Catholic reaction and political circumstance prevented further expansion and, in the end, Reformed survival was an unlikely achievement. Once facing repression, the theology of Calvinism suited revolution in that the doctrine of predestination and the theory of the elect brought with it a conviction that Calvinism would ultimately triumph over the forces of evil and that persecution was merely a test of God's will. To some, the Calvinist ethic was an arrogant and self-satisfied one, yet the certainty of faith held by the elect gave a sense of purpose to their actions.

However, to argue that Calvin fostered a religion of revolution would be false, as he essentially preached pacifism, stating that tyrannical rulers had to be endured and that only the nobility might intervene, thus suggesting that Calvin wished to avoid armed conflict, as we can see when Calvin delayed the setting up of consistories in France and did not attend the 1559 national synod, believing that the rulers of France could still be won over. Therefore, Calvin might advocate only passive resistance but, under harsh persecution, such theories were not likely to last and more aggressive ones were developed by Beza and Duplessis Mornay, which suited the political and military situations. Indeed, in some ways, Calvin's emphasis on noble leadership led Calvinists into conflict in both France and the Netherlands. French Calvinism was noble in character up until 1572, when over 200 of them were massacred in Paris and, as a consequence, the movement became more bourgeois and radical. Yet conversely, without the noble support of men such as Condé or Coligny, Calvinism would never have survived, just as the leadership of Orange and Maurice were important in the Netherlands, offering military and financial aid. Therefore, one might argue that Calvinism had to adapt to the political and military circumstances in France and the Netherlands, inevitably becoming a religion of revolutionaries and emerging relatively successfully as a minority faith in both as a consequence of discipline, organisation and zeal.

In Scotland, the Reformed faith emerged on the back of a political revolution involving the French, while even in Geneva one can talk of a political revolution in which Calvin sought to separate Church and State. Indeed, in all of these countries and everywhere in which Calvinism made an impact, there was a social revolution in which moral and religious standards were closely monitored by the consistory. Nowhere could replicate the Geneva of the 1550s and 1560s, but the way in which Calvinism was adapted by countries such as the Netherlands or Scotland had a lasting effect on the social, political and economic development of these states.

A2 ASSESSMENT

ESSAY QUESTIONS FOR CALVIN AND CALVINISM TO 1572

How to write an essay

To be awarded top marks in essays of the type given below, you will be expected to do the following:

- **Analyse throughout the essay.** This can be done by making sure you plan a line or argument before you start writing. At the start of each paragraph you must make the next point of your argument, explain it and then use evidence to back your point up (see next point). There is a clear difference between narrative (telling the story) and analysis (putting forward a reasoned argument in response to a question).
  A tip for how to ensure that you are analysing. You need to start each paragraph with words that will lead on to analysis. These might include: 'The most important reason'; 'Another key point is that'; One should argue that'; 'Essentially. . .'. If you use the following words at the start of a paragraph you are more likely to fall into a narrative style of writing: 'In (followed by a date)'; 'This was followed by . . .'.
- **Back up your argument by using well-selected evidence.** The evidence you select must be accurate and relevant to the point you are trying to make.
- **Make a clear and consistent attempt to reach a judgement.** In your essay you must argue throughout. You must reflect on the evidence you have given and make points that answer the question directly.
- **Show evidence of independent thought.** You do not have to be original. Independent thought means that you have reflected on what you have read in this and other books and that you can explain the ideas that you have picked up in your own words.
- **Language skills.** It is essential that you write in paragraphs and that you are grammatically accurate. There are two tips to ensure this takes place:
  - Always read your work through after you have finished and correct any errors.
  - Get into the habit of structuring your essays in such a way that a new point of your argument means a new paragraph.

Questions in the style of Edexcel from Unit 4: Calvin and Calvinism to 1572

The examination board will ask different styles of questions. Here are some examples:

Judgement questions

> **Question 1.** 'Calvinism appealed only to a social minority in Europe in the period up to 1572.'
> How far do you agree with this view?   (30 marks)

General points of advice. When answering judgement questions be careful that you:

- Make sure you offer a judgement. Whatever you do, you must argue rather than simply tell the story. A narrative-based answer is not appropriate.
- You must argue explicitly in support of the judgement you have made. The language you might use to do this is explained above.
- Do not 'sit on the fence' if you are being asked to decide between judgements.
- Try to sustain your judgement throughout the essay. Do not simply make your judgment at the end.
- There is no right and no wrong. If you support your judgement with evidence you will be rewarded accordingly.

Plan. This is clearly a question that provokes an 'up to a point…but' answer. Before you answer the question, you have to plan as thoroughly as you can.

Style. Throughout your essay you need to write in as direct as style as possible. The key is that you argue your case, explain your argument, back your argument up with information and reiterate the point. Here is an example from the start of a paragraph from a response to the question above. Note how the candidate remains direct in her response.

> *It is clear that, in some circumstances, Calvinism appealed to a wider social audience. In urban areas, the moral discipline of the new theology attracted converts from a range of trades and occupations. Nowhere was this more apparent than in Geneva. This support was reinforced by the support of the French refugee population, which became crucial in consolidating Calvin's position. Only one of the ministers on the Company of Pastors was not French and, as time passed, many of the lay elders were also selected from the French population. The unstinting support they offered Calvin after 1546 placed Calvin in a strong position when he fell into dispute with the council, because the latter could not risk civil unrest or the mass resignation of the Company.*

Here is another example:

Question 2. 'Calvin's success in Geneva was due to the organisation and discipline of the movement rather than his theology.' How far do you agree with this statement?

One-part causal questions
These are straightforward questions that ask you to analyse one aspect of Calvin's life and work, in this case his success. One should answer these questions with prioritisation.

- Argue that one factor you have identified is more important than any of the others.
- Link this factor to other factors that help explain why something happened.

Here is an example of a one-part causal question:

Question 3. Why was Calvin successful in Geneva, 1536–55?

Two-part causal questions
These types of question ask you to analyse two aspects of Calvin's work and life. In order to get full marks, you need to ensure you do the following.

- Plan the answer to both parts of the essay. If your plan looks at both aspects of the answer then you will have balance in your response.
- When answering the question, make sure you write a substantial amount about both parts of the question. The split does not have to be 50:50, but should be close enough.

Here is an example of a two-part causal question:

Question 4. Why were some attracted to Calvinism yet others strongly opposed his ideas?

BIBLIOGRAPHY

T.A. Brady, H.A. Oberman and J.D. Tracy (eds), *Handbook of European History 1400–1600* (Eerdmans Publishing 1995)

S. Brigden, *London and the Reformation* (Oxford 1989)

Euan Cameron, *The European Reformation* (Clarendon Press 1991)

A.G. Dickens, *The Counter Reformation* (Thames and Hudson 1968)

B. Diefendorf, *Beneath the Cross: Catholics and Huguenots in Sixteenth Century Paris* (Oxford and New York 1991)

G.R. Elton, *Reformation Europe 1517–1559* (Blackwell 1963)

Mack Holt, *The French Wars of Religion 1562–1629* (Cambridge 1995)

J. Lotherington, *Years of Renewal* (Hodder 1998)

D. Luebke, *The Counter-Reformation* (Blackwell 1999)

G. Parker, *The Dutch Revolt* (Penguin 1977)

A.D.M. Pettegree, *The Reformation in the Parishes* (Cambridge 1990)

A.D.M. Pettegree, *The Early Reformation in Europe* (Cambridge 1992)

A.D.M. Pettegree, *Emden and the Dutch Revolt* (Oxford 1992)

A.D.M. Pettegree, A. Duke, Gillian Lewis (eds), *Calvinism in Europe 1540–1670* (Cambridge 1994)

A.D.M. Pettegree, *The Reformation World* (Routledge 2000)

R. Po-Chia Hsia, *The World of Catholic Renewal 1540–1770* (Cambridge 1998)

Martyn Rady, *From Revolt to Independence 1550–1650* (Hodder 1987)

K. Randall, *Luther and the German Reformation* (Hodder 1988)

Jasper Ridley, *John Knox* (Oxford 1968)

Natalie Zemon Davies, *Society and Culture in Early Modern France* (Stanford 1975)

INDEX

Alva, Duke of 124
Amboise, Edict of 123
Anabaptists 59, 66–73
Assisi, St Francis of 77
Augsburg, Confession of, 1530 53–4
Augsburg, Interim of, 1548 57–8
Augsburg, Religious Peace of, 1555
   37–8, 50, 58–9, 93
Augustinian order 24

baptismal names 147
Barnabite order 76
Basle, Council of 84–5
Bergerac, Peace of 128
Bible in English 12
Bible in German 39–40
Body of Christ, The 64–5
Bolsec, Jerome 144
Borromeo, Carlo 97
Boulogne, Edict of 126–7
Bourbon family 116, 118
Bucer, Martin 139–40
Bugenhagen, Johannes 39, 58

Cajetan, Cardinal 25
Calvin, John
  background 68–73
  France 115–6
  Geneva 137–50
  predestination 71–2, 73
  Strasburg 139
  theology 71–3
Calvinism
  church structure 72
  France 114–9
  Geneva 136–50
  Germany 165
  Huguenots 116, 126–7
  Netherlands 152–63
  Religious Peace of Augsburg 59
  popular appeal 166
  religion of revolution 165–7
  Scotland 163–5
Campion, Edmund 101
Capuchins, The 77–8

Carlstadt, Andreas 34–5, 37–8
Casimir, John of 124
Catholic Church
  authority challenged 11
  co–existence with Lutheranism 59
  corruption 2–3, 8–11
  Eucharist, The 5–6
  financing 8
  humility 76
  Inquisition 101–4
  Jesuits as reformers 99–101
  reaction to Protestantism 104–5
  reform before the Council of Trent
    74–6
  reform, need for 8–11
  Renaissance, impact of 12–3
  sacraments, the 5
  simplicity 76
  social position 3–8
Catholic League 128, 130
Charles V, Emperor 29–31, 43–5,
  52–3, 56, 84, 89
communes 35
Company of Pastors 136, 143
conciliarists 85–6
Congregation of the Index 103, 104
Consilium delectorum
    Cardinalium......Ecclesia 87–8
consistory 141–2, 149
Constance, Council of 84–5
Contarini, Gasparo 75–6
conventicles 166
Cop, Nicholas 70
Counter Reformation 74

Divine Providence, doctrine of 116

Ecclesiastical Ordinances 73, 136,
   138, 140–1
Eck, Johannes 25–6
Edinburgh, Treaty of 163–4
Erasmus, Desiderius 12–3, 48, 58,
  83
Eucharist, The 5–6, 64–5, 89
excommunication 142

Farel, Guillaume 137
Felix, Treaty of 128–9
Ferdinand, Emperor of Austria 50–1
Four Cities Confession 65
France 45, 54, 82–3, 85–6
  Calvinism 114–9, 151–2
  Wars of Religion 97–8, 115, 117,
   119, 120–31, 161
Frederick III, Elector of Saxony,
  'The Wise' 31–2, 38, 45
Frederick III, Elector of the Palatine
  165

Gallicanism 119
Geneva 136–50
Genevan Academy 114
German States 56
Ghent, Pacification of 160
Guise, Charles, Cardinal of Lorraine
  95

Habsburg, Royal House of 10, 44
Henry IV of Navarre, King of
  France 130
Henry VIII, King 14, 86
Hoffmann, Melchior 67
Holy Roman Empire 29, 30, 42–3
Huguenots 116, 126–7
humanism 12–4, 48, 61, 70, 83–4
Hundredth Pennies 156
Hus, Jan 3,4, 11, 25–6, 29

Iconoclasm 153–4
Imperial Knights 46
Indexes of Forbidden Books 98,
  102, 103
indulgences 19–25
Inquisition 101–4
Institution de la Religion Chrétienne
  70–1, 136, 139, 152

Jesuits, The (Society of Jesus)
  78–80, 99–101

Kappel Wars 63

Kempis, Thomas à 80
Knox, John 163–4

Lateran Council, Fifth 86
League of Dessau 51
League of Torgau 51
Leiden, Jan van 68
Libertines 147
Lollards 12
Lords of the Congregation 163
Loyola, Ignatius 78–80, 101, 103
Luther, Martin
  background and chronology 3–4,
    16–7
  burning of papal bull 26
  comparison with Zwingli 63–5
  death 56–7
  declining influence 60
  early years 18–9
  flexible message 41
  indulgencies 19–25
  Ninety–Five Theses 20–4
  portraits 58
  sacraments, the 28
  theology and writings 26–9
Lutheranism
  expansion 49–60
  impact on a town 47–8
  popular movement 38–47
  princely support 38, 45–7, 49–50
  role of Martin Luther 38–9
  setbacks 34–8
  successes 34–8

Marburg Colloquy, The 53
Margaret of Parma 152–3, 154
Mary Queen of Scots 163–5
Medici, Catherine de 117
Melanchthon, Philip 39, 40, 53, 58,
  146
Mennonites 68
Monsieur, Peace of 127–8
More, Thomas 14
Morone, Cardinal Giovanni 95
Mühlberg, Battle of 50, 57, 59
Münster, Siege of 67–8
Müntzer, Thomas 36–7, 67

Nantes, Edict of 131
Netherlands 152–63
Nicodemism 115

Nonsuch, Treaty of 161
Nuremburg, Religious Peace of 54

Ochino, Bernardino 77
Oratory of Divine Love, The 75–6
Ottoman Empire 45

Parma, Duke of 160–2
Passau, Treaty of 58
Peasants' Revolt, The 35–8, 49
Perpetual (Bloody) Edict 152
Perrin, Ami 142, 143, 146–7
Philip II, King of Spain 156–63
Philip of Hesse 56–7, 65
Popes
  appointed 1484–1655: 85
  papal reform 84–8
  poor behaviour 9–10
  Alexander VI 9
  Clement VII 86
  Gregory XIII 98–9
  Julius II 86
  Julius III 90, 92–3
  Leo X 9–10, 20, 24–6, 86
  Paul III 87, 88–90, 91–2
  Paul IV 75, 93, 103
  Pius IV 94–6
  Pius V 98, 103
  Sixtus IV 102
  Sixtus V 99
predestination, doctrine of 71–2, 73
Presbyterianism 73
princely influence 38, 45–7, 49–50,
  82–4
Puritanism 73

Regensburg, Colloquy of 89

sacraments, the 5, 28, 72
Sadoleto, Jacop 87–8
St Bartholomew's Day Massacre
  125–6
St Germain, Treaty of 124
Savonarola, Girolamo 9
Schmalkalden Articles, The 55
Schmalkaldic League 54–5, 56
Schmalkaldic War 56
Scotland 73, 163–5
Sea Beggars 159
Sevetus, Michael 144–6
sin 6

Sixteen, The 129, 130
Sixty–Seven Theses 62
Somaschi order 76, 77
Song of Songs, The 144
Spain 95, 155–63
Speyer, First Diet of 45, 51–2
Speyer, Second Diet of 52
Spiritual Exercises 80
Staupitz, Johannes von 18
Swiss Confederation 62–3
synod 151

Tenth Penny, The 156
Tetzel, Johann 20, 23–4
Theatine order 76–7
Thiene, Cajetan da 76
To the Christian Nobility of the
  German Nation 37
transubstantiation 72, 89
Trent, Council of
  background 88–90
  ending 96
  implementation of decrees 97–9
  importance 90
  opening 89–90
  sessions 91–5
  significance 96–7
Twelve Articles of Memmingen 36
Twelve–Year Truce 162–3

United Provinces 152–63
Ursulines, The 80–1

Valois, Royal House of 10, 118
Vernazza, Ettore 75
Viret, Pierre 143

War of the Three Henris 129–30
William of Orange, Prince 154–5
Wittenberg Concord 55, 65
wonderyear [1566] 153
Worms, Edict of 29–31, 32, 36,
  50–1, 52
Wyclif, John 11–2

Xavier, Francis 100–1
Ximenes, Cardinal 82

Zurich 61–5
Zwickau Prophets 34
Zwingli, Huldrych 28, 53, 61–5